A HISTORY OF THE
NORTHERN SECURITIES CASE

Da Capo Press Reprints in

AMERICAN CONSTITUTIONAL AND LEGAL HISTORY

GENERAL EDITOR: LEONARD W. LEVY

Claremont Graduate School

A HISTORY OF THE
NORTHERN SECURITIES CASE

By B. H. Meyer

DA CAPO PRESS • NEW YORK • 1972

Library of Congress Cataloging in Publication Data

Meyer, Balthasar Henry, 1866-1954.
  A history of the Northern Securities case.

  (Da Capo Press reprints in American constitutional
and legal history)
  Reprint of the 1906 ed., which was issued as no. 142
of the Bulletin of the University of Wisconsin and
vol. 1, no. 3, of the University's Economics and
political science series.
  Bibliography: p.
  1. Northern Securities Company. I. Title.
II. Series: Wisconsin. University. Economics and
political science series, v. 1, no. 3.
KF2379.N6M48   1972   343'.73'095   70-124898

ISBN 0-306-71989-4

This Da Capo Press edition of *A History of the Northern Securities Case* is an unabridged republication of the first edition published in Madison, Wisconsin, in 1906 as No. 142 of the *Bulletin of the University of Wisconsin*. It is reprinted by permission from a copy of the original edition in the collection of the Alderman Library, University of Virginia.

For purposes of convenient reference, the pagination of the first edition has been retained throughout in square brackets.

Published by Da Capo Press, Inc.
A Subsidiary of Plenum Publishing Corporation
227 West 17th Street, New York, New York 10011

Manufactured in the United States of America.

A HISTORY OF THE
NORTHERN SECURITIES CASE

BULLETIN OF THE UNIVERSITY OF WISCONSIN

NO. 142.

ECONOMICS AND POLITICAL SCIENCE SERIES, VOL. 1, No. 3, PP. 215-350

A HISTORY OF THE NORTHERN SECURITIES CASE

BY

BALTHASAR HENRY MEYER, Ph. D.

*Professor of Political Economy in the University of Wisconsin and Member of the
Railroad Commission of Wisconsin*

*Published bi-monthly by authority of law with the approval of the Regents
of the University and entered at the post office at
Madison as second-class matter*

MADISON, WISCONSIN
JULY, 1906

TABLE OF CONTENTS.

APPENDICES.

CONTENTS.

PREFACE.

The first six chapters of this monograph, embracing about three-fourths of the whole, were ready for the printers in January, 1904, waiting for the decision of the Supreme Court. This decision was rendered on March 14, 1904, but since the first decision did not end the case, the essay was withheld from publication at that time. A summary of it was published in The Railway Age for March 18, 1904, Vol. xxxvii, No. 12, pages 409–412. For various reasons, it does not seem feasible at this time to change those expressions of the first six chapters which clearly indicate that they were written in anticipation of the first Supreme Court decision. The reader is requested to bear this in mind in reading those chapters.

The aim of this history of the Northern Securities Case is to present, in connected form, the leading facts and principles which may have an interest to students of economics, in so far as these principles and facts are contained in the record, briefs, and arguments of the Case. These embrace nearly 8000 pages in all. No attempt was made, excepting a few instances, to go outside of or beyond the statements made under oath by the various witnesses and the interpretations placed upon such statements by attorneys and judges. Several minor litigations connected with the Northern Securities Company have been practically ignored, for the reason that the chief records of such cases were embodied in the documents connected with the larger contest which these pages attempt to describe. A number of the briefer and more noteworthy documents are printed in the appendix to this essay.

B. H. MEYER.

Madison, Wis., January, 1906.

PRINCIPAL REFERENCES.

For convenience and brevity, the majority of the foot-notes and other references in the body of this monograph are generally given by number, each number corresponding to the same number in the following list of documents:

1. C. C. of U. S. Dist. of Minn. State of Minn. vs. North. Sec. Co. et al. Brief for the Defendants. (George B. Young, M. D. Grover, C. W. Bunn.)

2. C. C. of U. S. for the 8th Circuit. U. S. of A. vs. North. Sec. Co., N. P. Ry. Co., J. P. Morgan, James J. Hill and others. Oral Argument of James M. Beck, Asst. Atty. Gen. for the U. S.

3. C. C. of U. S. Dist. of Minn. State of Minn. vs. North. Sec. Co. et al. Defendants' Abstract—Evidence and Authorities.

4. C. C. of U. S. U. S. of A. vs. North. Sec. Co. et al. Brief for Morgan, Bacon and Lamont. (F. L. Stetson and David Wilcox.)

5. C. C. of U. S. U. S. of A. vs. North. Sec. Co. et al. Brief for the Northern Sec. Co. (John W. Griggs.)

6. C. C. of U. S. U. S. of A. vs. North. Sec. Co., G. N. Ry. Co., N. P. Ry. Co., and others. Brief for the N. P. Ry. Co. (C. W. Bunn.)

7. C. C. of U. S. U. S. of A. vs. North. Sec. Co., G. N. Ry. Co., etc. Brief for the G. N. Ry. Co. (M. D. Grover.)

8. C. C. of U. S., etc. Oral Argument of C. W. Bunn, at St. Louis, March 20, 1903.

9. Supplemental Brief by C. W. Bunn.

10. C. C. of U. S. State of Minn. vs. North. Sec. Co. et al. Brief of Complainant. (W. B. Douglas, Atty. Gen. of Minn., M. D. Munn, G. B. Wilson.)

11. C. C. of U. S. U. S. of A. vs. North. Sec. Co. et al. Brief for Defendants. (George B. Young.)

12. C. C. of U. S. State of Minn. vs. North. Sec. Co., etc. Volume of Pleadings.

13. S. C. of U. S. State of Minn. vs. North. Sec. Co. Bill of Complaint. (Douglas, Munn, Wilson.)

14. C. C. of U. S. Spec. Exam. Trans., Vol. III. Defendants' Testimony.

15. C. C. of U. S. Spec. Exam. Trans., Vol. 14, Defendants' Testimony.

16. C. C. of U. S. Spec. Exam. Trans., Vol. I, Complainants' Record.

17. C. C. of U. S. Spec. Exam. Trans., Vol. II, Complainants' Record.

18. C. C. of U. S. Spec. Exam. Trans., Vol. I, Complainants' Testimony.

19. C. C. of U. S. Spec. Exam. Trans., Vol. II, Complainants' Testimony.

20. S. C. of U. S. State of Minn. vs. North. Sec. Co. Complainants' Brief in Motion for leave to present and file bill of complaint.

21. S. C. of U. S. State of Wash. vs. North. Sec. Co., etc. Bill of Complaint. (W. B. Stratton.)

22. S. C. of U. S. Complainants' Brief, etc. (Stratton and Douglas.)

23. Memoranda of points and authorities for defense.

24. Interstate Commerce Commission. Order and Testimony.

25. C. C. of U. S. U. S. of A. vs. North. Sec. Co., etc. Oral Argument of D. T. Watson for the Government, at St. Louis, March 20–21, 1903.

26. S. C. of U. S. Oct. Term, 1903, No. 433. State of Minn. vs. North. Sec. Co., etc. Brief on behalf of appellant.

27. S. C. of U. S. Oct. Term, 1903, No. 277. Oral Argument of George B. Young.

28. S. C. of U. S. Oct. Term, 1903, No. 277. Brief for the U. S.

29. S. C. of U. S. Oct. Term, 1903, No. 277. Oral Argument of Atty. Gen. for the U. S.

30. S. C. of U. S. Oct. Term, 1903, No. 277. Brief for appellant, Great North. Ry. Co.

31. S. C. of U. S. Oct. Term, 1903, No. 277. Brief for North. Sec. Co. et al., Appellants.

32. S. C. of U. S. Oct. Term, 1903, No. 277. Brief for appellant, North. Pac. Ry. Co.

33. C. C. of U. S. Dist. of Minn. Memorandum as to alleged impracticability of restoration of the Status Quo.

34. C. C. of U. S. 3rd Dist. of Minn. Petition for leave to intervene and notice of presentation.

35. C. C. of U. S. Dist. of N. J. In Equity. E. H. Harriman, etc., Complainants, vs. North. Sec. Co. and N. P. Co., Defendants. Second Amended Bill.

36. C. C. of U. S. Dist. of N. J. In Equity. Notice of Motion, Order, Bill of Complaint, and Affidavits.

37. C. C. of U. S. Dist. of N. J. Brief on behalf of Complainants in support of motion for preliminary injunction.

38. C. C. of U. S. Dist. of N. J. Reply Brief in behalf of Complainants.

39. Depositions and Affidavits submitted for Defendant, North. Sec. Co.

40. Supplementary memorandum of points and authorities for defendant, North. Sec. Co.

41. Opinion by Bradford, J., granting preliminary injunction.

42. U. S. C. C. of Appeals, 3rd Circuit. North. Sec. Co., Appellant, vs. E. H. Harriman et al., Appellees. Brief on behalf of Appellees. (Dillon, Lovett, Evarts.)

43. Brief for the Appellees. (Watson.)

44. Brief for Appellant, North. Sec. Co.

45. S. C. of U. S. Oct. Term, 1904 No. 512. Brief on behalf of Petitioners and Complainants, Harriman et al., Petitioners and Complainants, vs. North. Sec. Co., impleaded with North. Pac.

46. Brief for North. Sec. Co.

47. Brief on behalf of Appellants.

48. Brief for Respondent.

49. Decision of the U. S. Supreme Court.

Since the monograph was written, the various decisions have been published in the customary manner, and the leading references are given below:

Decision of Trial Court, April 9, 1903.   120 Fed. Rep., 721.

First Decision of Supreme Court, March 14, 1904.   193 U. S., 197.

Decision of Circuit Court, April 19, 1904, denying leave to intervene. 128 Fed. Rep., 808.

Decision of Circuit Court, July 15, 1904, granting preliminary injunction.   132 Fed. Rep., 464.

Decision of Circuit Court of Appeals, January 3, 1905, reversing the order.   134 Fed. Rep., 311.

Final Decision of the Supreme Court, March 6, 1905.   197 U. S., 244.

A HISTORY OF THE NORTHERN SECURITIES CASE.

CHAPTER I.

GENESIS OF THE IDEA OF A HOLDING COMPANY.

The certificate of incorporation of the Northern Securities Company was signed by the three incorporators and acknowledged in the state of New Jersey on the twelfth of November, 1901. During the three days immediately following, resolutions were adopted by the newly organized company, authorizing the purchase of any shares that might be tendered to the company, under specified conditions and terms.[1] Power to do so was expressly granted in the charter. "The objects for which the corporation is formed are: To acquire by purchase, subscription, or otherwise, and to hold as investment, any bonds or other securities or evidences of indebtedness. . . To purchase, hold, sell, assign, transfer, mortgage, pledge, or otherwise dispose of, any bonds or other securities or evidences of indebtedness created or issued by any other corporation. . . To purchase, hold, etc., shares of capital stock of any other corporation . . . and, while owner of such stock, to exercise all the rights, powers, and privileges of ownership, including the right to vote thereon . . ."[2] The nature of these powers, with respect to the signs of indebtedness of other corporations, has caused the company to be commonly described as a holding company.

This particular idea of a holding company antedates the

---

[1] Proceedings, Board of Directors, 14 : 910-913.
[2] Certificate of Incorporation, Article 3.

Northern Securities Company by seven or eight years;[3] and, in a larger sense, the principle involved in the holding company has found at least partial expression in the organization of railway companies for half a century. The voting trust may also be regarded as an antecedent of the modern holding company, and the causes which have produced the one are analogous to those which have produced the other. The process of metamorphosis between the voting trust and the holding company does not appear to be either long or complex.

Both the remote and the immediate causes of the organization of the Northern Securities Company were partly personal and partly economic. They were personal in so far as the Securities Company was the outgrowth of a desire on the part of certain men to perpetuate a certain policy. They were economic in that the execution of certain large, almost empire-building plans could be promoted, in the estimation of its founders, by the Company. The founders of the Company, through years of effort, had become accustomed to associate their railway properties with a certain economic policy. And thus the personal and the economic causes of the organization of the Company practically become merged into one, namely, the desire to insure uninterrupted progress in the building of a great system of transportation. The existence of other causes, like the desire to suppress competition, to inflate values, has been alleged. An examination of these will be taken up later.

The original idea of the Securities Company was that it should embrace the ownership of about one-third of the Great Northern stock. A small number of the Great Northern stockholders, not to exceed eleven out of about 1800,[4] felt that they were getting along in years. One of them was eighty-six, another eighty-two, and several of them past seventy years of age; and they desired to work together as they had done for more than twenty years. Some of these stock-holders lived in foreign countries. Their powers and privileges had to be exercised by their legal representative. This might continue to work satisfactorily as long as the old circle of associates remained unbroken; but a number of them felt that a more per-

---

[3] Hill, Testimony, 24 : 43; see also 1 : 18; 2 : 21, 40; 3 : 41, 56, 60, 68; 4: 3; 10: 8, 9; 14: 698; 16 : 422; 17 : 436–440, 499, 502, 545; 18 : 191, 194, 197.

[4] Hill, Testimony, 14 : 698.

manent arrangement would be preferable. A close corporation, embracing six or eight men, was suggested, to which
others objected because such an arrangement would violate
the principle of equality which had always prevailed among
Great Northern stock-holders. As soon as the idea of ex-
clusiveness had been abandoned and an inclusive organization decided upon, "the question came up: Why not put in
the Northern Pacific? That is the way it occurred."[5] This,
in substance, is the manner in which President J. J. Hill
summarizes what has been alluded to above as the "personal"
element in the organization of the Securities Company. And
to place at the head of the new company the guiding spirit
and constructive genius of that group of men at once made the
Securities Company doubly a matter of "moral control,"[6] of
"fortification," and of "strength."[7] In the words of a col-
league, who is familiar with the territory through which the
Great Northern railway runs, that road is "regarded as a personality. People know that there is some one whom they can
see and talk to. If other means fail, they know they can
go to see 'Jim' Hill about it, and he will give them a fair hearing." From the three-fold point of view of public policy,
of personality, and of business, the actual course of the organization represents the best that could have been done.[8]

The desire to secure a permanent basis for the interchange
of commodities between great producing sections of the
United States and of the Orient may be characterized as the
largest economic cause of the organization of the Securities
Company. The Great Northern and Northern Pacific railways had lived in comparative peace with each other for
twenty years.[9] Both had maintained joint rates with other
roads like the Burlington. The Burlington taps[10] the principal live-stock markets, important cotton, coal and mineral
areas of the United States. The unified control and management of these three great systems of railways,—Great Northern, Northern Pacific, and Burlington—makes it possible to

---

[5] Clough, Testimony, 14: 814; Kennedy, Testimony, 16: 363; Hill, Testimony, 24: 50.
[6] Morgan, Testimony, 3: 70.
[7] Hill, Testimony, 24: 76.
[8] See also 23: 15-19; 16: 205-209; 389; 17: 454, 658.
[9] Hill, Testimony, 24: 72.
[10] Hill, Testimony, 14: 671, ff.

secure a sufficient variety and quantity of freight to make systematic back-loading a certainty. Back-loading, together with a steady flow of freight large enough to insure the economical utilization of motive power and car capacity, results in a general economy of operation which makes rates that would bankrupt numerous other roads remunerative to the systems embraced in the Securities Company. Such a flow of freight had been developed on the basis of joint rate agreements with railways and agreements with steamship lines. The value of the railway properties concerned, as well as the continued prosperity of the commercial and industrial interests served by them, depended largely upon the permanency and security of the arrangements which had begun to crystallize with the turn of the century, and to which the opening of the Orient promised to bring still greater returns.[11] However, joint rates may be withdrawn at any time, and it was thought too hazardous to build up a great business "extending across the continent and even across the ocean on the basis that tomorrow the rate might be changed or the party with whom we were working to reach the different points of production or consumption had some other interest or some greater interest elsewhere. It was necessary in doing this that we should have some reasonable expectation that we could control the permanency of the rate and that we would be able to reach the markets. In other words, if the man producing lumber on the coast, or cattle on the ranches, or ore in the mines, could not find a market for it and if we could not take it to a market that would enable him to sell his stuff for a profit, he would have to stop producing it. That was the line we worked upon, and that was the reason we felt called upon to put ourselves in a position where we could control access to the markets."[12]

---

[11] See Appendix 2 for the first cargo list of the S. S. "Minnesota."
[12] Hill, Testimony, 14 : 670–671.

CHAPTER II.

IMMEDIATE CAUSES OF THE ORGANIZATION.

A glance at a railway map[13] of the territory west of the Mississippi reveals the importance and strength of the Burlington system. West of the Missouri river it lies in the very lap of the Union Pacific, while east of that river it forms a great bridge, with its terminal pier in Chicago. The Northwestern, St. Paul and Burlington systems largely complement each other in the great manufacturing, agricultural and mineral regions of the greater northwest. In relation to the Great Northern and Northern Pacific, the Burlington is like the point and moldboard of a plow, the beam and handles of which are constituted by the former systems. The Burlington connects Chicago with St. Louis, Kansas City, Omaha, Denver, St. Paul and Minneapolis, and numerous smaller but important cities, which, taken collectively, represent the manufacture and sale of every staple commodity and the raw materials therefor.[14]

An alliance with a system possessing the tactical and physical advantages of the Burlington could not be otherwise than a source of strength and profit to the party making such an alliance.

For many years the Great Northern and Northern Pacific had been contemplating direct connection with Chicago. The usual alternatives of the construction of a new line or the lease or purchase of an existing one, presented themselves. The former would result in unnecessary duplication and waste; the latter only was deemed expedient. The improved

---

[13] Good maps are found in 14: 969; 17: 814, 900; 19: 504-662. One of these is reproduced in Appendix 10 to this monograph.

[14] A multitude of statements bearing upon the Burlington may be found in 3: 15; 11: 16-28; 14: 671-674, 685, 696; 16: 56-78; 17: 528, 536.

financial condition of the Northern Pacific and the dissolution
of the voting trust planned for January 1, 1901, made the year
1900 propitious for the execution of the long cherished plans
for an eastward extension. At least five different lines were
within the range of possibility. These were: the Wisconsin
Central; Chicago & Northwestern; Chicago, Milwaukee & St.
Paul; Chicago, Burlington & Quincy; and the Chicago Great
Western. To what extent each of these great lines figured as
possibilities in the minds of the Great Northern and Northern
Pacific, and the relative degrees of desirability which were attached to each by them, does not appear in the testimony,
although the statement may be positively made that more than
two of these railways were made the subject of correspondence and probably, also, of tentative solicitation.[15]

The preferences of J. J. Hill and J. P. Morgan, with respect to the particular line to be acquired as an eastward extension, do not appear to have coincided,[16] when an extraneous
factor appeared, which probably added the force of circumstances to Hill's preference. It appears that during the "fall
of 1900 or early winter of 1901" the Union Pacific interests
purchased in the market some $8,000,000 or $9,000,000 out of
$108,000,000 or $109,000,000 of the Burlington stock.[17] Much
of the Burlington stock had been held for many years by
people who had inherited it,[18] and it was found impossible to
secure control of the property through purchases in the open
market. This episode in the stock-market hastened the com-
pletion of negotiations which probably had been begun before
that time. The two northern transcontinental lines were not
inclined to permit a rival interest to wrest from them this
much coveted property without leaving a single stone un-
turned. The testimony does not show a direct causal connection between the attempt of the Union Pacific interests to
purchase the Burlington in the open market and the negotiations of Hill for the same property, although more than mere
coincidence probably existed. Negotiations were opened by
Hill with the executive committee of the board of directors of

[15] Private correspondence.
[16] Young, Brief, 11: 17. Morgan, Testimony, 17: 529.
[17] Hill, Testimony, 16: 74-75.
[18] Hill, Testimony, 16: 76.

the, Burlington system about Christmas, 1900, or January 1, 1901. Prior to this date no negotiations had taken place. "The actual negotiations commenced about or after the middle of January, 1901."[19] Early in March, 1901, E. H. Harriman and Jacob H. Schiff, acting for themselves, or for the Union Pacific, or for interests friendly to the Union Pacific, requested to be allowed to join with the Great Northern and Northern Pacific in the purchase of the Burlington.[20] This request was refused. At that time the Union Pacific interests no longer owned the eight or nine millions of Burlington stock which had been purchased during the preceding fall or winter, but they now desired to secure a half interest in the final purchase. A month later the Burlington sale was consummated. The two northern roads had made the offer which the Burlington directors had specified beforehand as satisfactory to Hill, and nearly all the Burlington shareholders accepted it.[21] The Great Northern and Northern Pacific each received one-half of the $108,000,000 of capital stock of the Burlington at $200 per share, payable in joint collateral four per cent, long time bonds of the two companies,[22] for the payment of which the acquired 96.79 per cent. of the stock of the old Burlington Company, was pledged as collateral security.[23] These two companies had now become joint owners of all the Burlington stock, and, as such, they had the right thereafter to exercise all the rights and privileges of shareholders, including the right to elect the board of directors. The purchase of the Burlington stock by the two companies in equal parts, it was thought, would serve each of them as well as if it were the sole owner of such stock, while such a purchase might have been beyond the financial means of either company by itself. "The evidence is therefore uncontradicted and conclusive that the Great Northern and Northern Pacific companies each purchased an equal number of shares of the Burlington stock as the best means and for the sole purpose of reaching the best

---

[19] Hill, Testimony, 16: 57–58.

[20] Hill, Testimony, 16: 77.

[21] Various reports regarding the manner in which certain stockholders were induced to part with their stock are in circulation, but I have been unable to confirm them.

[22] 19: 505–545, contains copies of the bond, etc.

[23] Hill, Testimony, 16: 67; Beck, Argument, 2: 23–27.

markets for the products of the territory along the lines, and of securing connections which would furnish the largest amount of traffic for their respective roads, increase the trade and interchange of commodities between the regions traversed by the Burlington lines and their connections and the regions traversed or reached by the Great Northern and Northern Pacific lines, and by their connecting lines of shipping on the Pacific Ocean, and as the best if not the only means of furnishing an indispensable supply of fuel for their own use and for the inhabitants of the country traversed by their lines. These connections and the interchange of traffic thereby secured were deemed to be and are indispensable to the maintenance of their business, local as well as interstate, and to the development of the country served by their respective lines, and of like advantage to the Burlington lines and the country served by them, and strengthen each company in its competition with European carriers, for the trade and commerce of the Orient."[24]

During the very days when the Burlington transaction was being perfected, the men who had been refused what they regarded an equitable share in that purchase elaborated plans which were calculated to vanquish their enemies and elevate the Union Pacific interests to a position of supremacy in transcontinental traffic. These stirring events led a cosmopolitan editor to invent a parable of fishes in which the bass had swallowed the minnow, and the pike swallowed the bass. In this instance, however, the bass, armed with retirement fins, compelled the pike to spew him out.

The total outstanding capital stock of the Northern Pacific was $155,000,000 of which $80,000,000 was common and $75,000,000 preferred. During April and early in May, 1901, the Union Pacific interests acquired $78,000,000 of this stock,— $41,000,000 preferred and $37,000,000 common—with the view of controlling the Northern Pacific railway, with its half interest in the Burlington system. Such a movement appears to have been anticipated. "It was a common story at one time."[25] Individuals representing the Great Northern and

24 Young, Brief, 11 : 21.
25 Morgan, Testimony, 17 : 536.

Northern Pacific interests, becoming apprehensive, increased their holdings in the Northern Pacific by purchasing about $15,000,000 of common stock in the market.[26]   Short selling of Northern Pacific stock and the scramble to cover, when it was discovered that only a limited supply was to be had, drove the price of Northern Pacific common stock up to about $1,000 per share.   This was the climax of a series of events which culminated in the stock-exchange crisis of May 9, 1901.[27] "The markets of the world were convulsed, the equilibrium of the financial world shaken, and many speculative interests in a critical condition."[28]   On May 1, 1901, when the so-called "raid" upon Northern Pacific stock became known, J. J. Hill and his associates, who had been in possession of large blocks of Northern Pacific stock from the time of the reorganization of the company, were holding from $18,000,000 to $20,000,000, par value, of common stock; and J. P. Morgan & Co. were holding some $7,000,000 or $8,000,000.[29]   Together, May 1, 1901, these individuals lacked the dramatic $15,000,000 of common stock, which, when they had acquired it, gave them a majority of some $3,000,000 par value, and of the $80,000,000 of common stock, when the "show down of hands" occurred after May 9.   Although the Union Pacific interests represented by E. H. Harriman and Winslow S. Pearce, as trustees for the Oregon Short Line, held a majority of $1,000,000 of the total amount of stock, their majority lay in the preferred shares which could be retired on any 1st of January prior to 1917,[30] —that is, before the present owners could get an opportunity of exercising the authority which was assumed to reside in them, and which would give them the coveted control.   This is why the pike did not swallow the bass.   To the country at large and to Wall Street these events appeared like a duel be-

---

[26] Morgan, Testimony, 17 : 539.

[27] Some competent spectators did not regard the Northern Pacific corner and the preceding events which were directly connected with it as the cause of the panic of May 9. "It was the concurrent condition of the money market that gave an atmosphere of desperation to the general surroundings." Banks were unable or unwilling to extend accommodations, loans had to be called, the public had engaged in wholesale speculation, etc. All these things combined to increase the intensity of the popular craze. See the *Commercial and Financial Chronicle*, Vol. 72:744, 842, 900, 903, 958.

[28] Beck, Argument, 2 : 30.

[29] Young, Brief, 11 : 31-32; Hill, Testimony, 16 :78-81; Nichols, Testimony, 16 : 325-332.

[30] Resolution of Board of Directors, 17 : 879.

tween giants, but one who appears to have been a leading participant in the duel, on the losing side, asserted that he never was in a contest,[31] nor did he and his associates lose money.[32]

According to the by-laws of the Northern Pacific Company, the annual election of its board of directors by the stockholders occurs in October, and under the distribution of stock existing after May 9, 1901, the Union Pacific interests could have controlled this election, and thus prevented the retirement of the preferred stock on January 1, 1902, which would legislate them out of control. Both the preferred and the common stock could vote under the conditions existing on May 9, 1901. A postponement of the annual meeting from October till after January 1, 1902, was frequently thought of and advised by counsel. It could have been done.[33] This potential power of retiring the Northern Pacific preferred stock before the same could be voted, residing in the Northern Pacific Board of Directors, appears to have generated a conciliatory attitude on the part of the representatives of Union Pacific interests, and negotiations for the purchase of such shares were successfully carried through by J. P. Morgan & Co. Direct testimony admitting this causal connection does not exist, but the admitted facts make it appear highly probable. To be sure, the retirement of the preferred stock had been thought of long before, and the right to do so on any 1st of January between 1896 and 1917 was expressly reserved;[34] yet up to 1901, when this plan was finally consummated, no plan had been devised for the retirement of that stock.[35] The interested parties agreed not to wait until October, but to act at once, in order to establish permanent peace and "to show that there was no hostility."[36] The detailed movements[37] following the 9th of May do not appear clearly from the evidence, but the results of what took place are indicated in the bulletin published on June 1st. "It is officially announced that an understanding has been reached between the Northern

[31] Harriman, Testimony, 19: 612, 618.
[32] Harriman, Testimony, 19: 616.
[33] Young, Brief, 11: 33; Hill, Testimony, 16: 134–138; Morgan, Testimony, 17: 542.
[34] Resolution, 17: 879.
[35] Morgan, Testimony, 17: 567.
[36] Morgan, Testimony, 17: 542.
[37] Hill, Testimony, 16: 123–131; Morgan, Testimony, 17: 545.

Pacific and the Union Pacific interests, under which the composition of the Northern Pacific board will be left in the hands of J. P. Morgan. Certain names have already been suggested, not now to be made public, which will especially be recognized as representative of the common interests. It is asserted that complete and permanent harmony will result under the plan adopted between all interests involved."[38] This "understanding" had been incorporated in the Arbitration Agreement of May 31, 1901, which the bulletin just quoted announced to the public, and which gave "every important interest its representative." In it the "vitality and vigor of the peace policy established between the railroads" found definite expression.[39] It showed "that they were acting under what we know as a community of interest principle, and that we were not going to have that battle in Wall Street. There was not going to be people standing up there fighting each other."[40] Had this battle in Wall Street been fought to the last ditch and the Union Pacific interests triumphed, the measure of the injury done to the Great Northern and Northern Pacific would have been destruction, in the judgment of those who are responsible for the administration of these properties,—destruction in the sense that the properties would have been incapacitated from doing what it was intended they should do and what they were quite able to do[41] in building up a great interstate and Oriental traffic, unless they had all gone into a single combination. "With the Northern Pacific as a half owner in the shares of the Burlington and responsibility for one-half of the purchase price of these shares, the transfers of the shares of the Northern Pacific or the control of the Northern Pacific to an interest that was adverse or an interest that had greater investments in other directions, the control being in the hands of companies whose interests would be injured by the growth and development of this country would, of course, put the Great Northern in a position where it would be almost helpless, because we would be, as it were, fenced out of the territory south which produces the tonnage we want to take

---

[38] Beck, Argument, 2 : 34.
[39] *Com. & Fin. Chronicle*, Vol. 73 : 104, 978.
[40] Morgan, Testimony, 17 : 543, 569 ; Harriman, Testimony, 17 : 569.
[41] Hill, Testimony, 14 : 693–697, 742.

west and which consumes the tonnage we want to bring east, and the Great Northern would be in a position where it would have to make a hard fight—either survive or perish, or else sell out to the other interests. The latter would be the most business-like proceeding." With the view of preventing the possibility of future "raids" upon the Great Northern and Northern Pacific stock and of fortifying these two roads and their connections in their competitive struggle with "the Suez Canal and the high seas and the entire world,"[42] the idea of a permanent holding company was invented. It has been persistently denied that the desire to restrain competition among the constituent companies had anything to do with the organization of the Northern Securities Company.[43]

---

[42] Hill, Testimony, 14: 695.
[43] The question of competition will be taken up specifically in Chapters V and VI.

CHAPTER III.

THE ORGANIZATION.

The organization of a holding company having been determined, it was necessary to decide upon the form and contents of a charter, or articles of incorporation, and the state in which the incorporation should take place. The general nature of the contents of such a charter had been discussed practically as long as the idea of a holding company had been entertained by the men interested in the matter;[44] namely, for something like seven or eight years. The specific nature of such a charter for this particular company was not made the object of study until after the Arbitration Agreement of May 31, 1901. About this time several men began an examination of the laws of a number of states for the purpose of discovering a suitable charter and of deciding upon the state in which the company should be incorporated. The decision with reference to the place of incorporation was not made until a few days before the company was actually incorporated.[45] The general aim in searching for a charter and a state "was to have beyond any question the power to purchase, own and hold and dispose of corporate securities on a large scale."[46] Between June and October several different sketches of articles of incorporation were made[47] and submitted to seven or eight men. These men were scattered so that no formal meeting for the consideration of the articles was ever held.[48] The sketch referred to left blank the name of the corporation, the name of the state in which it was to be incorporated, and the amount of the capital stock. "There was practically no change in the

---

[44] Clough, Testimony, 14 : 819.
[45] Clough, Testimony, 14 : 826, 831.
[46] Clough, Testimony, 14 : 829.
[47] Beck, Argument, 2 : 48.
[48] Clough, Testimony, 14 : 821, 829.

substance of it from the beginning."[49] Among the earliest
efforts was a search for a special charter granted by the territory of Minnesota prior to the adoption of the constitution of
1858. "A large number of special charters that were passed
when Minnesota was a territory have been very much sought
after and extensively used by railroads that have since been
built, by financial institutions of various kinds and business
corporations."[50] The old enactments were glanced through
with a view of seeing if there was anything that would meet
the desires and purposes of the contemplated organization, because "under our constitution all charters ante-dating the admission of the state into the union became fixed legislative
contracts."[51] Such a special, territorial charter could, however, not be found; nor could a later charter suitable for the
occasion be discovered. Hence, recourse was had to the general incorporation laws of Minnesota, New York, New Jersey,
and probably also of West Virginia.[52] The Minnesota statutes were regarded as too "new in that class of corporations.
There are no large business corporations incorporated under
the laws of the State of Minnesota; she never has had any.
There has been no occasion to put powers that are given by
her general statutes to such organizations under judicial question."[53] Furthermore, her own citizens, it was asserted, go to
other states for the incorporation of enterprises of any magnitude.[54] Whether West Virginia was any more than mentioned in this connection does not appear. As between the
statutes of New York and New Jersey, the choice fell upon
the latter because they had been in force a good many years
and were regarded as "thoroughly well settled." Those of
New York, on the other hand, while they were quite similar to
those of New Jersey, and "had evidently been passed with a
view of enlarging her legislation to put it on a parity with
New Jersey," were of very recent origin, and had not been
construed by the courts.[55] In this connection, reference may

---

[49] Clough, Testimony, 14 : 828.
[50] Clough, Testimony, 14 : 817–818.
[51] Clough, Testimony, 14 : 817.
[52] Clough, Testimony, 14 : 824.
[53] Clough, Testimony, 14 : 830.
[54] Young, Brief, 11 : 57.
[55] Clough, Testimony, 14 : 825.

be made to a pamphlet entitled "Advantages of the General Corporation Act of New Jersey,"[56] published without reference to the Securities Company, in which the author of it points out that since 1846 the policy of New Jersey towards capital has been that of "liberality." The changes introduced in the law since then have made it "simpler, more liberal and less burdensome. Since 1896, when the law was again revised and codified, its salient features have been simplicity of organization and management, freedom from undue publicity in the private affairs of the company, and facility of dissolution."[57]

The charter, which was finally taken out in the state of New Jersey, is in many respects similar to the charters of other great corporations. It has many points in common with the charters of the United States Steel Corporation, and the Standard Oil Company, except that the Northern Securities charter does not grant the omnibus powers conferred by the others. The Standard Oil Company and the United States Steel Corporation can engage in practically every conceivable kind of enterprise, while the Northern Securities charter limits the company to the acquisition of valuable paper held by domestic and foreign corporations, exercising the rights of property over the same, aiding corporations whose paper is thus held, and acquiring and holding the necessary real and personal property. The amount of the capital stock with which the corporation began business was thirty thousand dollars, while the total authorized capital stock of the corporation is four hundred million dollars. The customary officers and committees are provided for and the usual powers conferred upon them.[58] A board of fifteen directors was elected, six of whom represented Northern Pacific interests; four, the Great Northern, not counting the president; three, the Union

---

[56] Published by the Corporation Trust Company.
[57] Leading references on the search for a charter:
    Brief for Defendants, 1 : 19;
    Beck, Argument, 2 : 42–60;
    Brief of Complainant, 10 : 18, 45;
    Young, Brief, 11 : 57;
    Clough, Testimony, 14 : 820–844; 16 : 238, 253, 318;
    Morgan, Testimony, 18 : 354.
[58] The by-laws are printed in 17 : 804–814.

Pacific; and two, unclassified.[59] The composition of the board on the community of interest plan was one of the points of attack subsequently pursued by the state and federal authorities. Such an arrangement had numerous precedents, however. Chauncey M. Depew is an officer or director of fifty-six transportation companies; W. K. Vanderbilt of fifty-one; Geo. J. Gould of thirty-five; E. V. Rossiter of thirty-one; E. H. Harriman of twenty-eight; Charles F. Cox of twenty-seven; D. S. Lamont of twenty-four; J. P. Morgan of twenty-three, and so on through a list of more than a hundred names.[60]

Much testimony was elicited with respect to the capitalization and the ratio at which the Northern Pacific and Great Northern shares were exchanged for Northern Securities stock.[61] It seems that the capitalization of $400,000,000 was fixed at that figure in order to cover approximately the combined capital stock of the Northern Pacific and Great Northern at an agreed price apparently based upon earning capacity. The par value of the outstanding capital stock of the Great Northern was $123,880,400.00 and that of the Northern Pacific amounted to $155,000,000.00. The Northern Securities Company purchased about seventy-six per cent of the former and ninety-six per cent of the latter, on the basis of $115.00 per share of $100 of Northern Pacific and $180.00 per share of $100 of the Great Northern. The purchase of the stock of the two railway companies by means of the shares of the Securities Company was effected by and through the stockholders as such. An offer to make the purchase was conveyed to the Great Northern stockholders in a circular letter.[62] This circular called forth numerous inquiries, in response to which President Hill sent out a letter[63] setting forth the purposes of the company and suggesting that "the offer of the Securities Company is one that Great Northern shareholders can accept with profit and advantage to themselves." It was the expressed wish of the leading stockholders of the Great Northern that all of them should be dealt

[59] See table, 2 : 59; 17 : 814; 24 : 136–138.
[60] Compiled from the Directory of Directors for New York, 1902.
[61] Leading references upon this point: 10 : 4–6; 14 : 789, 910–20; 16 : 79, 119–144, 168–183, 324–350, 416; 17 : 532–554, 575; 24 : 58–64; 25 : 78.
[62] Printed, 14 : 918
[63] Printed, 14 : 920.

with on a basis of absolute equality, irrespective of the amount of their holdings. This appears to have been done. In case of the Northern Pacific no circular letter appears to have been sent out to stockholders;[64] nor were the same rules of equality applied to them, for the Union Pacific interests received a cash premium of $8,915,629.00 in the exchange of their Northern Pacific holdings on the agreed basis for $82,492,871.00 par value of the Northern Securities stock. It also seems that the promoters of the Northern Securities Company had an understanding with the holders of at least a majority of the common stock of the Northern Pacific Railway Company that they would exchange that stock for the stock of the Northern Securities Company as soon as organized; and also an agreement that the preferred stock of the Northern Pacific should be retired on the first day of January following.[65]

---

[64] Such a letter is, however, implied in Volume of Pleadings, 12 : 35.
[65] Complainant's Brief, 10 : 41.

CHAPTER IV.

ACTION OF THE STATE AUTHORITIES.

One week after the Northern Securities charter had been granted, the following statement was issued from the office of Governor Van Sant of Minnesota:[66] "Owing to the great interest of the people of the states west of us and of the great desire to see the attempt to consolidate the Great Northern and Northern Pacific Railway lines resisted, Governor Van Sant has concluded to invite the Governors of the states having anti-consolidation laws similar to those of Minnesota to join in an effort to fight the great railway trust. It is understood that a conference of the governors is to be planned to consider the best methods of fighting the Northern Securities Company's propositions in the courts and by new legislation, if necessary." The replies of the governors addressed varied. The governor of North Dakota stated that his state had very little law bearing upon the question. In the constitution the consolidation of parallel and competing lines is specifically prohibited, and there are some general enactments prohibiting the formation of trusts and pools for the purpose of hampering trade and commerce. The governor of South Dakota thought that the railways in the merger had so little mileage in his state that any action there would be of no moment. The absence of constitutional provision or law in Idaho caused the governor of that state to regret that he could consequently render no material aid in the contest, but he thought that the matter would be made the subject of action by the next legislature. When Oregon repealed her commission law in 1898, practically all railway legislation was wiped out with it. The governor of Oregon wrote Governor Van Sant that the people

[66] Quoted, *Com. & Fin. Chron.*, Vol. 73, p. 1112.

MEYER—HISTORY OF THE NORTHERN SECURITIES CASE.

of that state were so well satisfied with the treatment that they had received from the railways that the legislature had ignored his recommendation in two successive messages that the anomalous condition as to the control of railroads be changed. The governor of Washington replied that his state had a clause in its constitution prohibiting general monopolies, but no special provision as to the union of railways. However, he promised hearty co-operation to the extent of his ability. The governors and attorneys-general of the states mentioned held a conference at Helena, Montana, on December 31, 1901, and unanimously adopted the following resolution: "In our opinion the consolidation or threatened consolidation of the Great Northern, Northern Pacific, and Burlington Railway systems in the several states through which they run as parallel or competing lines is contrary to sound public policy, and also, with the exception of Idaho, is in violation of the constitution or laws of said states, and mindful of the obligation which the law imposes in such cases upon the officials of the several states here represented, we hereby give our unqualified approval and indorsement to any proper and suitable proceeding which may be instituted in any court having jurisdiction by the sovereign state of Minnesota, or any other state affected thereby, designated, designed, and intended to speedily and finally test and determine the validity of such consolidation or threatened consolidation. And further, we unanimously protest against any combination or consolidation which restricts or stifles free competition in the trade or commerce of the country."

One week later, namely, on January 7, 1902, Attorney-General Douglas of Minnesota, in behalf of the state, appeared before the supreme court of the United States and moved the court for leave to file a bill of complaint against the Northern Securities Company. The court[67] answered that "the general rule in equity is that all persons materially interested, either legally or beneficially, in the subject-matter of a suit, are to be made parties to it; and the established practice of courts of equity to dismiss the plaintiff's bill if it appears that to grant the relief prayed for would injuriously affect per-

---

[67] 184 U. S., 199–247.

sons materially interested in the subject-matter who are not made parties to the suit, is founded upon clear reasons, and may be enforced by the court, *sua sponte*, though not raised by the pleadings, or suggested by counsel.

"The bill discloses that the parties to be affected by the decision of this controversy are, directly, the state of Minnesota, the Great Northern Railway Company, and the Northern Pacific Railway Company, corporations of that state, and the Northern Securities Company, a corporation of the state of New Jersey, and, indirectly, the stockholders and bondholders of those corporations, and of the numerous railway companies whose lines are alleged to be owned, managed or controlled by the Great Northern and Northern Pacific Railway Companies; and it is obvious that the rights of the minority stockholders of the two railroad companies are not represented by the Northern Securities Company."

The denial of the court is expressed in the concluding paragraph of the decision in the following language: "As then, the Great Northern and the Northern Pacific Railway Companies are indispensable parties, without whose presence the court, acting as a court of equity, cannot proceed, and as our constitutional jurisdiction would not extend to the case if those companies were made parties defendant, the motion for leave to file the proposed bill must be and is *denied*."

This decision of the supreme court was rendered on February 24, 1902. Thereupon the attorney-general of the state of Minnesota brought suit in the state court. The bill alleged a right of recovery under the Sherman Anti-Trust Act, contending that as a shipper the state could maintain an action under the federal act. This, it was thought, gave a right of removal to the United States circuit court, where the suit was tried. The state of Washington also applied to the United States supreme court for leave to file a bill in that court. Such leave was granted, the bill was filed, and the defendants answered. Nothing further was done in that case.

The case of the state of Minnesota against the Securities Company is outlined in the brief of complaint and volume of pleadings before the United States circuit court for the district of Minnesota, and in the bill of complaint before the

United States supreme court. The action was brought by the state of Minnesota "in its capacity as a governmental or sovereign body on behalf of all the people of the state, and also in its individual or corporate capacity for the purpose of enjoining the consolidation of the Great Northern and Northern Pacific Railway companies."[68]

In its individual capacity, it was argued, the state is a landowner and shipper. As a sovereign body, the state sought to enforce compliance with its statutory and constitutional provisions relating to the consolidation or combination of competing or parallel lines of railway and to combinations in restraint of trade. It sought a vindication of "the majesty of its own laws."[69] Minnesota has an anti-trust law which is essentially like the federal anti-trust law of 1890 in so far as it forbids contracts, combinations or conspiracies in restraint of trade; and since a discussion of the federal law constitutes the chief topic in the part of this monograph dealing with the action of the United States government, no extended reference to arguments upon this point of the case is necessary here. The statutes which particularly come under consideration in this place are the following: "No railroad corporation, or the lessees, purchasers or managers of any railroad corporation, shall consolidate the stock, property or franchise of such corporation with, or lease or purchase the works or franchise of, or in any way control any other railroad corporation owning or having under its control a parallel or competing line, nor shall any officer of such railroad corporation act as an officer of any other railroad corporation owning or having the control of a parallel or competing line."[70] And again, "No railroad corporation shall consolidate with, lease or purchase, or in any way become the owner of or control any other railroad corporation or stock, franchises, rights, or property thereof, which owns or controls a parallel or competing line."[71] The Great Northern Railway was chartered by the state of Minnesota, while the Northern Pacific was originally chartered by the federal government

---

[68] Brief of Complaint, 10 : 1, 112.
[69] Same, 10 : 115.
[70] Sec. 1, Ch. 29, Laws of Minn., 1874, quoted, 10 : 2.
[71] Laws of 1881, quoted, 10 : 2.

and later re-chartered by Wisconsin; but having subsequently filed its charter in Minnesota, both railway companies were clearly within the jurisdiction of the state. The question of jurisdiction was not an important point at issue.[72] The crucial point in reference to the two Minnesota laws quoted is whether or not the Great Northern and Northern Pacific are parallel or competing lines within the state of Minnesota. Counsel for the state answered the question in the affirmative, these railways "having upwards of thirty junction points within the state and running generally parallel to each other, and only a very few miles apart, through a large portion of their extent in the state of Minnesota." A glance at the map will show that physically the two railways are clearly parallel with each other; at least, quite as parallel as scores of other roads generally regarded as being parallel. But aside from physical location, and with reference to traffic, counsel for the defense presented arguments showing that in reality only a small percentage of the total interstate traffic was competitive; and, in addition, the statement of Hill, previously referred to, that the two roads had lived in "unbroken peace"[73] with each other for about twenty years, with the exception of a threatened war which lasted only a few hours, should be recalled. No active, general competition was in existence at the time the Securities Company was organized. It was argued that less than three per cent of the total interstate traffic of the two companies was subject to control by them individually in the making of rates. In other words, ninety-seven per cent of the total interstate traffic of the two companies was being carried under joint tariffs, such tariffs being in force with eighteen railway companies west of the Missouri river and with 120 companies east of that river. The following is an analytical table of the traffic of the two roads:[74]

---

[72] The question was raised, however, and argued. See 10 : 94, ff.
[73] 24 : 67.
[74] M. D. Grover, Brief, 7 : 42–44.

MEYER—HISTORY OF THE NORTHERN SECURITIES CASE.

(a) The percentage of interstate traffic on the lines of the defendant companies which can be controlled by joint action of the companies is as follows:

Great Northern 2 78
Northern Pacific 2 89

Percentage of interstate traffic, the rates on which can be controlled by joint action of defendants with connecting lines:

Great Northern 65
Northern Pacific 4 90

Percentage of interstate traffic, the rates on which can be controlled only by agreement with lines competing with the defendants:

Great Northern 6 89
Northern Pacific 2 58

Percentage of interstate traffic, the rates on which can be controlled only by agreement with lines competing with defendant companies and with connecting lines:

Great Northern 17 09
Northern Pacific................................ 13 25

Percentage of interstate traffic moving between stations on line of Great Northern Company, neither of which is reached by lines of the Northern Pacific 72 59

Percentage of interstate traffic moving between stations on line of Northern Pacific Company, neither of which is reached by lines of the Great Northern............. 76 38

(b) Interstate business forwarded from and to towns reached by lines of the defendant railway companies only:

Great Northern $471,218 88
Northern Pacific 554,395 24

Total interstate business, both companies:

Great Northern $16,920,906 00
Northern Pacific 19,253,852 00

Making due allowances for the possibility of error, it seems reasonably clear that only an inappreciable portion of the total traffic is strictly competitive. To what extent this small percentage reacts, or can react, on the level of non-competitive

3

rates, through the action of the long and short haul clause, is a question which nothing but a detailed analysis of the total traffic by commodities can answer; and for this, the data are not at hand. It was the contention of the state that competition has been suppressed to the disadvantage of certain public and private interests. It was represented that the state of Minnesota now has left and unsold more than three million acres of public lands donated by congress and valued at fifteen millions of dollars. Much of this land is located in the regions traversed by the Great Northern and Northern Pacific railways, and its salability, as well as its market value, it was argued, depends in a very large measure upon the free and uninterrupted competition of the two railways. Nor will settlements be made as rapidly as heretofore, because such settlements depend largely upon the construction of branch lines into unsettled regions. The necessity for rivalry to secure the traffic of the new settlements no longer exists; and, all these things put together, will greatly retard the development of the more remote parts of the state. Again, the state is a shipper. It owns and maintains a university, hospitals, normal and industrial schools, schools for the deaf, dumb, blind, feeble-minded, indigent and homeless children. These institutions necessitate the purchase of large quantities of supplies, a great portion of which must be shipped over the lines of the Great Northern and Northern Pacific railway companies; and the absence of competition among the two railway companies may compel the state to pay higher rates and suffer the loss therefrom in increased taxation.[75]

The president of a normal school testified[76] that the agents of the two companies had visited his institution for the purpose of inducing students to travel between the school and their homes over their respective lines. In certain instances special cars, even, had been provided. This had not been done since the organization of the Securities Company.

Reference was also made to the large areas of land given by the state in aid of railways, which was met by counsel for the railways by the statement that the state of Minnesota had

---

[75] Pleadings, 12 : 18-24, 26, 36.
[76] 17 : 681-687.

acted only in a fiduciary capacity in regard to these lands by
executing a trust imposed upon it by the federal government;
and that the state could consequently not use arguments based
upon aid given through land grants.

The state claimed that "not only was all competition, so far
as rates were concerned, withdrawn or destroyed, but all effort to secure business and all the benefits resulting therefrom to shippers on the lines of said railroads within the state
of Minnesota, were absolutely destroyed; spur tracks and
sidings, which had been constructed in order to obtain competitive business and give conveniences and facilities to shippers on the Great Northern line who might otherwise ship
via the Northern Pacific were abandoned and removed and
shippers were left to get their grain and products to the
Railway Company as best they could; and when complaint
was made to the Great Northern Railway Company's agents,
accompanied with threats to transfer their business to the
Northern Pacific unless these conveniences were restored,
they were informed that it made no difference to the Great
Northern whether it or the Northern Pacific got the business."[77] The destruction of competition was partly attributed
to a joint circular letter, commonly spoken of as the equalizing circular, sent out to freight agents at nineteen junction
points on January 23, 1902.[78] The essential parts of this circular read as follows:[79] "Freight shipments from one junction point to another junction point, will be forwarded via
the line having the shorter mileage and lower rates; the
longer line will not undertake to equalize the rates based on
the shorter mileage of the other. Freight from a junction

---

[77] Brief, 10 : 15.

[78] Printed in 17 : 901.

[79] The freight circular relating to rates between junction points was issued principally because of the provision in the Minnesota law which forbids charging more for a
shorter than for a longer distance over the same line in the same direction on the same
class of freight. The law is absolute and does not contain the qualifying phrase of the
interstate commerce law "under similar circumstances and conditions." The Northern
Pacific Company, in making the same rate as the Great Northern between junction
points, was under legal obligation to make no higher rate from an intermediate point
to a junction point. The circular was issued because the company having the larger
line could not afford to adopt an intermediate rate as low as the rate made by a short
line between junction points. The Northern Pacific applied to the Commission for
leave to adopt the same rate between junctions as made by the shorter line, at the same
time maintaining a higher intermediate rate. This application was denied.

point destined to a local point on the other company's line
may be accepted if the joint rate made on the sum of the locals
of both companies is less than the rate of the company on
whose line the local point is located, for example,......Rates
made by combination of local rates will not include any transfer charges at junction points...." A witness was introduced
who testified[80] that after the issuance of this equalizing circular the choice of routes which he had enjoyed for five years
or more, at the same rates, had been denied to him, and that
the rate had also been advanced. The former privileges and
rates were restored through the withdrawal of the equalizing
order on March 27, 1902. Between the dates of issuance and
withdrawal of the circular, both the state and federal gov-
ernments were active in their suits against the Securities
Company, and counsel for the state draws the conclusion that
the withdrawal was due to the suits. Business considerations, however, entered into the question of the equalizing
circular which were not brought out in the testimony, as the
following statement by President Hill and the accompanying
map will show: "The equalizing circular enabled the Northern Pacific Railway Company to carry freight over its long
line at the short line rate of the Great Northern Railway. Mr.
Wright's testimony refers to shipments of caskets from Fergus Falls, Minn., to Moorehead, Minn. The distance via the
Great Northern Railway is 54 miles, and the rate 28 cents per
100 pounds. The Northern Pacific Railway Company under
its equalizing circular applied the 28 cent rate over its line,
a distance of 142 miles. On January 25th, 1902, the Great
Northern Railway and Northern Pacific Railway Companies
issued tariffs reducing the freight rates of merchandise about
15 per cent in Minnesota and the Dakotas. Under these revised tariffs the rates from terminal points, namely, St. Paul,
Minneapolis and Duluth were 95 per cent of the rates charged
on the same class of freight for the same distance from in-
terior points, such as Fergus Falls, etc. In order to carry out
this new principle establishing a fixed relation between the
terminal points and country shipping points, the application
of short line rates via circuitous routes was abandoned by

---

[80] Wright, Testimony, 17 : 675-681.

DIAGRAM I.

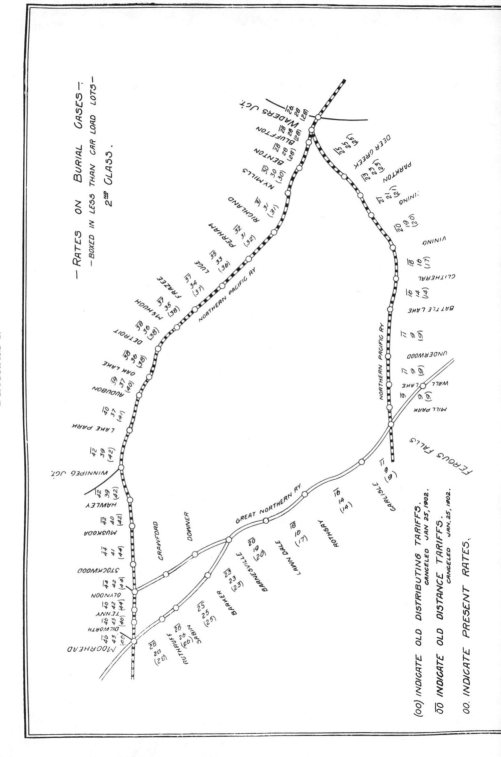

both the Northern Pacific and Great Northern Companies. This resulted in the Northern Pacific discontinuing the handling of freight shipments from Fergus Falls to Moorehead over their long line at the rate established over the Great Northern Railway. The attached memorandum[81] shows rates applicable on burial cases under the old and the new conditions. If the Great Northern and the Northern Pacific Companies had continued their previous practice of applying short line rates via circuitous routes, it would have resulted in establishing lower rates for the same service from country stations than we were charging from terminal points. This was considered objectionable, as the basis so applied might eventually be used as an argument for a further reduction in rates from the terminals."

Another witness[82] related that he had enjoyed the use of a spur and side-track of the Great Northern about one-third of a mile distant from his farm buildings, which was taken up after the organization of the Securities Company, compelling him to ship "from 10,000 to 15,000" bushels of wheat from another station about two and a half miles away on the Northern Pacific. When this siding was built, some fifteen years ago, the witness gave the right of way and the company provided the material. The witness also remarked concerning the decline of farm house solicitation for business on the part of the two railway companies. Special inquiries regarding the alleged changes in soliciting business and the abandonment of spur tracks and sidings elicited the reply that "no material changes have been made in our methods of soliciting traffic since 1900."[83] Farmhouse solicitation still exists. "It is confined principally to shippers delivering grain direct from the threshing machine to cars; the railway company endeavoring to learn the needs of such shippers in advance in order to furnish sufficient cars to avoid a suspension of threshing operations. Such farmers cultivate large areas, commonly termed 'Bonanza Farms' which are becoming fewer every year. Thus the necessity for this class of solicitation

[81] Consult Diagram I on opposite page.
[82] Addison Leech, 17 : 704–718.
[83] Private Correspondence.

is diminished correspondingly."[84] The matter of abandoned side-tracks was explained in the following manner:[85] "The only farmer's side track taken up by this company in years is the one mentioned in Leech's testimony. This track was built to accommodate the shipments of the Leech farm, when it occupied an area of about 8,000 acres. At that time Leech built an elevator at the end of the track, which was destroyed by fire about 1897, and not rebuilt. The farm having been greatly reduced in area, Mr. Leech evidently no longer considered an elevator necessary to accommodate his grain. Shortly after the destruction of this elevator, it developed that the track needed repairing, involving an expenditure of nearly $4,000.00, in order to put it in shape to handle cars with safety. Subsequent to the building of this side track, we located Addison Station at the junction with our through line. Elevators were built and a trading community established there, thus accommodating many of the farmers shipping from land previously owned by Leech. This deflection of business from Leech's spur to Addison Station with the gradual decrease in business controlled by Leech indicated clearly that we would not be justified in the expense necessary to continue the operation of this spur track and it was taken up." Two other witnesses[86] spoke of the greater difficulty at present encountered in securing empty cars and the comparative lack of promptness in having loaded cars taken away. "They ran their switch engine out once or twice with cars expressly for us this year. But heretofore they used to run their switch engine out pretty nearly every day."[87] The following remarks bear upon this point:[88] Various considerations affect the supply and movement of cars. Some grain shipping stations receive more cars under load with freight than others, thus providing to some extent cars for shipping grain. In many instances we are obliged to haul cars empty to shipping points, the time consumed in supplying them depending upon the distance transported. Some

---

[84] Private Correspondence.
[85] Private Correspondence.
[86] Ewald Weidemann and Theo. F. Koch, 17 : 719–731.
[87] 17: 729.
[88] Private Correspondence.

shippers have better shipping facilities than others and load more cars in a given time. Freight train service depending upon the volume of business is more frequent on lines where the traffic is greatest.

"Weidmann and Wagner in their testimony intimated that our company had discontinued soliciting their carload shipments of agricultural products. This was due to a change in our agents in Moorehead, Minn., under which the new agent neglected to pursue the method of solicitation of handling their business that had been followed by his predecessor. There was also a brief interval during the period covered by their testimony during which cars were very scarce and we were unable to supply them as promptly as in previous years. This was a temporary condition and has not existed since. The cars are promptly taken forward after they are loaded, excepting in cases where shippers fail to furnish shipping instructions promptly or when passing trains are unable to handle any additional cars. Such cases are an exception and not the rule."

Another argument related to shipments of grain and other products from competitive places in the western part of Minnesota to Duluth, St. Paul, and Minneapolis. It was shown that enormous quantities of such products, owned and produced by citizens and inhabitants of the state, were shipped to these markets. The destruction of competition, it was argued, would result in inferior service and increased rates.[89]

J. P. Morgan[90] "never knew two roads yet that didn't compete," but such statements can only be accepted in their loosest figurative sense. Competition as a regulative principle of railways and as a force which will maintain proper relations between the railways themselves and the railways and the public has failed in every country of the world where it has been given a trial, and on a priori grounds one would be obliged to assume, in the light of experience, what the analytical table of traffic illustrates, that no free and comprehensive competition did exist between the Great Northern and Northern Pacific railways; nor could such competition exist

---

[89] 13 : 5.
[90] Testimony, 17: 533.

in the long run. Hence, whatever may be said for and against
the Securities Company, it can scarcely be maintained that it
has affected the competitive relations of the two companies in
any substantial manner. In regard to the Burlington, these relations are said to have remained unchanged. Since the organization of the Securities Company, as before, both the Great
Northern and Northern Pacific authorities have "pestered"[91]
the Burlington for business from that road. This business has
been, and still is, divided between the two on a basis proportionate to the freight received by the Burlington from each, unless shippers order it routed otherwise.[92] In a word, then, the
Great Northern and Northern Pacific railways are parallel
and competing in so far as physical location is concerned, and
with respect to a relatively small part of their interstate traffic. They are not, and have not been, competitive with respect to any but an inappreciable part of their total traffic.
From the point of view of physical location, the two railways
are parallel, and if the purchase of shares of competing carriers by a single interest is forbidden by the law, which, it is
claimed is not the case, the law has plainly been violated. It
has also been violated from the point of view of potential or
"inactive" competition. If "competitive" railways, in the eyes
of the Minnesota law, are railways which compete for the
greater part or substantially all of their traffic, the law has
not been violated; but it has undoubtedly been violated if
"competitive" means competitive to any extent whatsoever,
and not competitive in regard to the whole of the traffic; provided that the purchase of the shares was in itself an illegal
act. If the courts should hold that unity of ownership of
shares is not a consolidation of the propery of the two railway companies it is difficult to see how the law can be made
to apply.[93]

---

[91] Darius Miller, Testimony, 17 : 617.
[92] Leading references for testimony relating to competition are:
    (1) 14; 697, 728, 733, 905, 910-913; 969.
    (2) 16: 25-40, 49, 166-178, 244, 411, 431-433.
    (3) 17: 505, 522, 529, 533, 547, 583, 596, 605, 607, 611, 616-644, 676-680, 695, 710-742.
    (4) 23: 10-13.
    (5) 24: 17, 51, 56, 57, 68-75.
[93] It should be recalled that this was written before the court decisions, as stated in
the Preface.

There is, perhaps, no fact connected with the history of the Northern Securities Company which is so vulnerable as the search for an old territorial charter which would be beyond the power of legislative amendment and not subject to general laws and constitutional provisions adopted since the granting of such charter.[94] To a layman who is incapable of inventing one complex set of legal technicalities to offset another set of technicalities, the mere attempt to organize a great corporation of the present on the basis of an ancient charter, granted at a time when present conditions could not have been foreseen and when corporate magnitudes of the

---

[94] A different view is expressed by Mr. M. D. Grover, General Counsel for the Great Northern Railway company, in the following statement:

"Mr. Clough testified as follows:

"It was thought desirable if a company was formed that it should have the stability that a charter beyond the power of legislative amendment would give, and such a charter should be acquired for it if possible. It was known that the territory of Minnesota before the admission of the territory into the Union had granted a great many charters for financial and other companies, and it was thought possible that some of those old charters could yet be found that would contain the powers that would be considered necessary for the purpose and that would at the same time be legislative contracts with the state of Minnesota so that they would be beyond the power of amendment."

"In this there was nothing objectionable or subject to criticism. An investment company was to be organized with a large capital for the purpose of holding shares it might purchase representing a very large investment and being valuable through securing a permanent business condition and relation. Permanency of conditions attending the obtaining of traffic and the building up of a large business is essential.

"Corporations have only such power as the states in which they are organized give them. Unless there is a provision in the charter to the contrary, all charters are subject to alteration and amendment, even to the extent of impairing invested rights. Charters are a contract between the state and the incorporators. If a charter is accepted subject to the right of the state to alter or amend it at any time the incorporators or stockholders cannot object because they have accepted it and assumed all the burdens and risk incident to the exercise of the power. A charter giving rights to engage in business requiring large capital and very large credit, is much more valuable where all vested rights are secured against alteration by repeal or amendment than charters subject at all times to legislative will and to the vicissitudes of politics.

"The paper in question correctly sets forth the reasons for adopting the state of New Jersey and a charter under its laws. The laws respecting corporations and large business interests have been enforced, not in a spirit of distrust and with a view to limit or destroy corporate privileges, but with a view of recognizing the security of property and of corporate rights to hold and dispose of property. Much of the discussion concerning consolidations and unity of property in single control goes only to the point of the power of corporations engaged in business and to have a capital much larger than can be commanded by individuals in the exercise of their individual business right. Whether corporations ought to be organized with as large powers as some of them possess is a question to be discussed with a view of influencing a consideration of the matter by the legislatures of the several states. Since corporations have only such powers as the states where they are incorporated give them and cannot, except as respects carrying on interstate commerce, engage in business in states other than where incorporated, unless given permission by other states, there is little likelihood of injury to the public through the organization of corporations as have heretofore been formed."

year 1901 could not possibly have been imagined, is a deliberate effort to evade both the constitution and the law. There are hundreds of old charters still lying about this country. It may be technically legal in most states to utilize them for the purpose of re-organizing great corporations of today; but no amount of legality can suppress the conviction that such action would violate the spirit of existing law and that it would be contrary to public policy and out of harmony with the spirit of the times. In Massachusetts, for instance, nearly all the railways operate under early private charters, but they have accepted the general laws enacted since, although the plea of an inviolable contract could easily be maintained against such acceptance.[95] Hence we are not surprised to have the attorney-general of Minnesota sarcastically refer to the search for a "place of incubation."[96] The feelings which this search have aroused are fully justified. Had an acceptable territorial charter been found with powers prohibited by subsequent enactments, the state of Minnesota would apparently have stood in conflict with itself—a tantalizing comment on our legislative methods and history. A New Jersey charter, argued the attorney-general, cannot be secured for the express purpose of violating the laws of another state; furthermore, the laws of New Jersey provide that corporations may be formed thereunder "for any lawful purpose."[97] If the purpose of such a charter is in contravention of the laws of the state in which the corporation does business, it becomes of no effect, even under the laws of New Jersey.

Other points brought forward by the state, especially those based upon the anti-trust law, will be discussed, as was suggested above, in connection with the federal case. The dedense, being generally alike for both cases, will be presented in its entirety in the same connection.

---

[95] The writer pointed out what he considered an illegitimate use of old railway charters in 1899, in a paper before the *American Economic Association*. See *Proceedings of Twelfth Annual Meeting of American Economic Association*, p. 232.

[96] Brief, 10 : 19.

[97] Brief, 10 : 95.

CHAPTER V.

ACTION OF THE FEDERAL GOVERNMENT.

The first public, official cognisance taken of the Northern Securities Company under federal law was a resolution of the Interstate Commerce Commission, adopted at a general session of the Commission in the City of Washington, D. C., on December 20, 1901, which reads as follows:

"'IN THE MATTER OF CONSOLIDATIONS AND COMBINATIONS OF CAR-
RIERS SUBJECT TO THE ACT TO REGULATE COMMERCE, INCLUDING
THE METHOD OF ASSOCIATION KNOWN AS THE 'COMMUNITY OF
INTEREST' PLAN.

"Whereas the twelfth section of the act to regulate commerce provides that the commission 'shall have authority to inquire into the management of the business of all common carriers subject to the provisions of this act, and shall keep itself informed as to the manner and method in which the same is conducted,' and requires the commission 'to execute and enforce the provisions of this act;'

"And whereas it appears to the commission that certain consolidations and combinations of carriers subject to the act, including the method of association known as the 'community of interest' plan, should be made the subject of investigation, to the end that the commission may be informed as to their formation, purposes, and modes of operation, together with their effects upon the movement of interstate commerce and the rates received therefor, and to the further end that it may be ascertained whether such consolidations, combinations, and methods of association are unlawful under the act or have the effect of violating any of its provisions:

"*Ordered*, That a proceeding of investigation and inquiry into and concerning the matters above recited be set for hearing at the United States court rooms, Monadnock block, in the city of Chicago, Ill., on the 8th day of January, 1902, at 10 o'clock a. m., the further hearing to be continued at such times and places as may appear to be required."

The Commission subsequently published the volume numbered "24" in the list of references of this essay. The testimony and documents contained in the same were later incorporated in the Special Examiner's Transcripts and made a part of the testimony on the Northern Securities case.

The next action on the part of the federal government was taken by the president of the United States when he requested Attorney-General Knox to express his opinion as to the legality of the procedure involved in the formation of the Northern Securities Company. On February 19, 1902, the attorney-general authorized the following statement to be published:[98] "Some time ago the president requested an opinion as to the legality of this merger, and I have recently given him one to the effect that, in my judgment, it violates the provisions of the Sherman Act of 1890, whereupon he directed that suitable action should be taken to have the question judicially determined." Accordingly, on March 10, the United States commenced suit in the United States circuit court at St. Paul against the three companies—Northern Securities, Great Northern, and Northern Pacific. Testimony was taken during October, November and December in St. Paul and New York. The case was argued before a special trial court at St. Louis, beginning March 18, 1903. This tribunal was composed of the four circuit judges of the eighth circuit, pursuant to the provisions of an act of congress approved on February 11, 1903,[99] which requires such cases to be heard "before not less than three of the circuit judges" of the circuit where the suit is brought if the attorney-general files with the clerk of the court wherein the case is pending, a certificate that it is one of "general public importance." Such a certificate was filed, and in accordance with the mandate of the statute the case was "given precedence over others and in every way expedited."[1]

---

[98] 2 : 63.

[99] Public—No. 82

[1] Opinion and Decree, p. 2.

The federal case against the Northern Securities Company was brought to enjoin the violation of the "Act to protect trade and commerce against unlawful restraints and monopolies" of July 2, 1890, commonly known as the Sherman Antitrust Act, and section 5 of the Interstate Commerce law. As was suggested above, the state case rested partly upon the same ground, because the Minnesota anti-trust law is identical with the federal law in so far as it forbids contracts, combinations or conspiracies in restraint of trade. "The record in the state case is in all material respects identical with the record in the government case. . . The relief sought in that case and in the state case is the same, namely, an injunction restraining the Northern Securities Company from holding and voting the stock of the defendant railway companies, and the railway companies from permitting the Northern Securities Company to vote their stock. The question in the government case and in the state case is whether the purchase by the Northern Securities Company of the shares of the defendant railway companies was, by reason of the voting power of the shares unlawful as in restraint of trade or a consolidation of competing railway companies."[2]

The representatives of the federal government rested their arguments in part upon the decisions of the United States supreme court in the Trans-Missouri and Joint Traffic cases.[3] They argued that *every* contract in restraint of trade, whether reasonable or unreasonable, was in violation of the law. "We cannot read the word 'unreasonable' into the act. Congress may put it there; we cannot. That is the province of congress, not of the court. The act says *all* restraint; it does not say all *unreasonable* restraint, but *all* restraint"[4] "Every person who shall monopolize or attempt to monopolize, or combine or conspire with any other person or persons, to monopolize any part of the trade or commerce among the several states, or with foreign nations, shall be deemed guilty of a misdemeanor," says the law. It forbids "three different crimes":[5] (1) monopolize; (2) attempt to monopolize; (3)

[2] M. D. Grover, General Counsel, in private letter.
[3] 166 U. S. 290 and 171, U. S. 505, respectively.
[4] Watson, Argument, 25 : 49
[5] Watson, Argument, 25 : 16.

combine, or conspire—"to breathe together"—with any other person or persons to monopolize. The possession of an actual monopoly is not necessary. The mere tendency to control is sufficient to stamp a combination as an illegal monopoly.[6] Nor is the active exercise of acquired monopolistic powers essential. The mere possession of such power is unlawful. More than that. The law forbids the obtaining of the power. "This breathing together to acquire the power" is in itself a conspiracy.[7] Furthermore, it is not necessary to prove that the Northern Securities Company intended to violate the law. Having demonstrated that a violation of law has been incurred, the manner in which it has been violated is immaterial. "In this case, the defendants cannot excuse themselves by saying: We did not intend to gain this power to stifle or cripple competition. It was not our purpose. We intended in the formation of this Northern Securities Company to form a benevolent corporation in which some aged men wished to put their stock in these railroad companies merely to keep it there."[8] "The benefit to the people of this merger may be all that its master spirit, Mr. James J. Hill, . . . claims it to be, . . .; it may accomplish 'vaster purposes in the development of traffic'; but these arguments of beneficent influences should be addressed to congress and not to the courts.[9] The powers of the Security Company are 'infinite in scope, perpetual in character, vested in the hands of a few', and may be exercised 'by methods secret even to stockholders.'[10] It will be interesting to follow out the possibilities of such a corporation. The original idea of the holding corporation, as explained by noted financiers, is to enable the minority to rule the majority. Thus, if two constituent companies have a joint capital of $100,000,000, it will take $51,000,000 to control them; but if a holding corporation can be formed and can acquire $51,000,000 of stock, then $26,000,-000 will dominate the holding corporation, which will in turn

[6] Watson, Argument, 25:16.
[7] Watson, Argument, 25:28.
[8] Watson, 25:34.
[9] Beck, Argument, 2:112–13.
[10] Beck, Argument. 2:57–8.

dominate the $100,000,000 corporation. Thus the quarter will dominate the three-quarters. This idea, however, is modest as compared with the Northern Securities Company, for, not only does a majority of the Northern Securities Company, namely, $201,000,000, control the Burlington, Northern Pacific, and Great Northern systems, and all subsidiary companies, whose aggregate capitalization, including funded debt, exceeds $1,000,000,000, but the board of directors, whose holdings of Northern Securities may be comparatively insignificant, can, during the tenure of their office, appoint a committee with power to act and to use the seal of the corporation at pleasure. This committee may be only three in number, and a majority is determinative. Thus, in the last analysis, two men may control the unlimited powers of the holding company, which, in turn, controls the vast powers of the Burlington, Northern Pacific, and Great Northern companies, and all subsidiary companies."

At this point it appears feasible to present in a more positive form several of the arguments in the federal case made by the representatives of the Securities Company.[11] The basis of a number of the economic arguments is found in the first two chapters of this monograph, namely, that the formation of the Northern Securities Company was necessary for the protection of property, made valuable through years of effort, against hostile interests; that no restraint, but rather an extension of commerce was intended; that an increase in traffic and a consequent reduction in rates would be effected; in short, that the Securities Company arrangement would result in advantages alike to the public and to the railways. The Securities Company, it was argued, was the result of a movement on the part of the stockholders, as such, of the constituent companies, and rested ultimately upon the right of the individual to purchase property to the extent of his wealth. In other words, the Securities Company was simply one expression of the rights of private property. "It is not a violation of the Anti-Trust Act for an individual to purchase or take by gift, marriage or inheritance all the shares of competing interstate carriers. A combination among all the

---

[11] Documents, 4, 5, 6, 7, 8, 9, 11.

holders of the shares of competing interstate carriers to sell their shares to any single interest is not a criminal combination. It is an agreement for the sale of property to one who has a right to purchase it. The sale is not interstate commerce. By such sale the rate making power of the corporation issuing the stock sold is in no respect limited or qualified. A holder of a majority of shares of a corporation engaged in interstate trade, whether as merchant, manufacturer, or carrier, may lawfully purchase in executive sale all the shares of a competing carrier. One owning a majority of shares of an interstate carrier may marry the holder of a majority of shares of a competing interstate carrier, and if by operation of law the personal property of a wife becomes the property of her husband, such shares of the wife would become the property of her husband, and his holding of the shares is not forbidden by the Anti-Trust Act because of his power to vote the shares at an election of directors of the respective companies. The holders of a majority of shares of the Great Northern Railway Company might have entered into a partnership with the holders of a majority of the shares of the Northern Pacific Company, and all their shares of stock in each company might have been lawfully transferred to the partnership and held by it as a partnership asset."[12] In opposition to this the government contended that no man has the absolute right to use his property as he sees fit. Its enjoyment has always been subject to restrictions. The law is full of limitations of its use. The right of property is no more sacred than the right to follow a trade or profession. "And the fundamental principle upon which it is all based is that we all form part of a great social whole, and that every man owes a duty to the whole. The individual welfare must yield to the good of the community. *Salus populi suprema lex.*"[13] Applying this to the Securities Company, it was argued that every purchase of the stock of the two railway companies was a step in the illegal purpose to control the two roads. The first purchase may have been entirely innocuous, and the second and third also; but when all the pur-

---

[12] Grover, Brief, **7**: 30–31; also Stetson and Wilcox, **4**: 16.
[13] Watson, Argument, **25**: 89; also 77, 87, 97.

chases necessary for control had been made the crime was committed, and every purchase was therefore made an unlawful act.[14] "If such a corporation as the Northern Securities Company, with like powers, is lawful today, with four hundred million dollars of capital stock, tomorrow it will be equally lawful with four billion dollars of capital stock. If, with four hundred million dollars it may buy the Northern Pacific and Great Northern, with four billion dollars it can buy the control of every other railroad in this country and become the absolute dictators as to the carriage of every pound of freight."[15]

In both the state and the government cases frequent references were made to the Trans-Missouri (166 U. S., 290), Joint Traffic (171 U. S., 505), and Addyston Pipe (175 U. S., 211) cases. The defendants maintained that these cases were not in point as respects the alleged combination to form the Northern Securities Company and transfer shares to it. In all these cases, it was argued, the corporations had agreed to do a specific thing—establish rates and prices—which in itself was unlawful. The Northern Securities Company is not an unlawful combination because it is a corporation organized to do a lawful act.[16] Neither does the Pearsall case (161 U. S., 646) apply, because in that case the Great Northern Railway Company made a contract with the bond-holders of the old Northern Pacific Company.[17] In the Securities case the constituent corporations have taken no action whatever. The result was attained solely through the action of the stockholders, "and it is settled by controlling authority that their rights and powers are entirely distinct from those of the corporation itself."[18] According to this doctrine, the action of a corporation is something distinct from the action of the stockholders composing the same, although the result may be substantially the same. The government admitted the existence of such a legal fiction, "but that the statement is a mere

[14] Watson, Argument, **25**: 41.
[15] Watson, Argument, **25**: 97. On June 30, 1901, the outstanding railway capital was $11,688,147,091.
[16] Grover, Brief, **7**: 35; Bunn, Brief, **6**: 14–20; Young, Brief, **11**: 109–136.
[17] Stetson & Wilcox, Brief, **4**: 5; Bunn, Argument, **8**: 24.
[18] Young, Brief, **11**: 166.

4

fiction, existing only in idea, is well understood, and not controverted by any one who pretends to accurate knowledge on the subject. . . . All fictions of law have been introduced for the purpose of convenience and to subserve the ends of justice. . . . But when they are urged to an intent and purpose not within the reason and policy of the fiction, they have always been disregarded by the courts. . . . So that the idea that a corporation may be a separate entity, in the sense that it can act independently of the natural persons composing it, or abstain from acting, where it is their will it shall, has no foundation in reason or authority, is contrary to the fact, and to base an argument upon it, where the question is as to whether a certain act was the act of the corporation, or of its stockholders, cannot be decisive of the question, and is therefore illogical; for it may as likely lead to a false as to a true result."[19]

Historically, the most interesting argument for the defense related to the development of railway combinations and the evolution of the holding company. It was contended that the consolidation of competing lines had been a matter of common knowledge before the passage of the Act of July 2, 1890; and that, if congress had intended, under the Act, to prohibit similar combinations in the future, the law would have given direct and definite expression to such a prohibition. Hence, congress did not intend to forbid, and does not forbid, "the natural processes of unification which are brought about under modern methods of lease, consolidation, merger, community of interest, or ownership of stock."[20] Besides, the Northern Securities Company is "not a railroad company, never had anything to do with the operation of railroads. The question of the purchase of the stock of two competing railroads by a third party has never been before the supreme court of the United States."[21] The last sentence has reference to the Trans-Missouri and Joint Traffic cases, in which, among other things, the court held that railways were included in the Act of 1890. The Northern Securities Company not being a railway company, it was argued, would not

---

[19] Beck, Argument, 2 : 90-91; Watson, Brief, 25 : 42-5.
[20] Griggs, Brief, 5 : 41; Young, Brief, 11 : 175-201.
[21] Young, Testimony, 14 : 885.

come within the scope of the Sherman law. Again, the Securities Company was represented as not being a "contract" or "combination," but only an investment or holding company, which would also exclude it from the operation of the law of 1890. The government took exception to these statements, asserting that the difference between a railway company and the Securities Company, between a technical merger and a transfer to the holding company, was "the difference between tweedle-dum and tweedle-dee."[22] "The whole transaction was nothing more than the exchange of pieces of paper for other pieces of paper, both being certificates of ownership; the buyers were the sellers and the sellers were the buyers, with this important difference, that the part owner of the property of the Northern Pacific Railway, or the Great Northern, found himself a part owner of the property of both. Had the two constituent companies formally consolidated, no different results would have been accomplished." The government objected to the introduction of Poor's Manual as irrelevant and immaterial,—an objection which was raised periodically by both sides with respect to nearly every part of the testimony. The government was unwilling "to have unloaded onto us the railroad history of the country from the beginning."[23] "Can a man charged with an offence when brought into court plead as a defense that others have been guilty of like acts?" It was, however, admitted on the part of the government that historical facts which enable the court to determine the conditions and circumstances congress had in mind when the Sherman Anti-trust law was passed, could consistently be introduced. Six hundred pages of historical material were introduced.[24] These facts of railway history stand out in strongest relief as a monument to the futility and inefficiency of anti-consolidation legislation and its administration in the United States. The railway system of the United States and legislation prohibiting consolidations of parallel or competing lines developed together,—but in opposite directions, independently of each other. The set of railway administrative inventors has always been a little

[22] Beck, Argument, 2 : 53.
[23] Richards, Solicitor, 14 : 882.
[24] Printed in 15.

ahead of the competing set of legislative legal inventors. The
following summary will illustrate this:[25]

"As early as the year 1840 three railroad companies were incorporated in the states of Massachusetts, New Hampshire and
Maine to build a line of interstate railway from Boston to Portland: the Eastern Railroad of Massachusetts, the Eastern Railroad in New Hampshire, and the Portland, Saco and Ports-
mouth Railroad Company. About that time the Boston and
Maine Railroad Company was incorporated in Massachusetts
to build a railroad from Boston to Maine. Long before the passage of the anti-trust act, the Boston and Maine had itself first
leased those parallel and competing lines, and afterwards practically absorbed all of them. So, again, some years before the
passage of the anti-trust act, the West Shore Railroad extended
from Weehawken in New Jersey to Buffalo, with ferry connections to New York, and was a competing line with the New
York Central. That line was leased by the New York Central,
and its entire stock of ten million dollars was acquired by
the New York Central and Hudson River Railroad Company;
and that was a matter of common knowledge and known to
congress when it passed the Sherman Anti-trust Act. In like
manner, the Lake Shore & Michigan Southern road, extending
from Buffalo to Chicago, formed with the New York Central and other roads, at Buffalo, a line of interstate railway between New York and Chicago. About the year 1881, a rival
and competing line, the New York, Chicago & St Louis,
known as the Nickel Plate Line, was projected and built between Buffalo and Chicago, having the same connections and
opportunities for interstate traffic that the Lake Shore itself
had, and was a rival and actually competing line; and the
majority of the capital stock of that company was acquired as
early as 1883 or 1884 by the Lake Shore and Michigan Southern Railway Company, thus making from New York to Chicago a series of parallel and competing lines, where the stock
of one system, or a majority of it, was owned by the railroad
which controlled the other system. In like manner the principal highways of interstate commerce between the cities of
New York and Philadelphia were originally a parallel rail-

[25] Young, Testimony, 14: 876–884.

road and canal; the Camden and Amboy Railroad, and the Delaware and Raritan Canal, chartered by the state of New Jersey prior to the year 1840. Prior to 1871, those systems had become closely united in operation with the road of the New Jersey Railroad & Transportation Company from Jersey City to Trenton, and the road from Trenton to Philadelphia known as the Philadelphia and Trenton. In 1871 the Pennsylvania Railroad Company leased perpetually all of those parallel and competing lines, and has ever since operated them between New York and Philadelphia. Prior to the year 1870 the Pennsylvania Railroad Company had a substantially perpetual lease of the railroad from Pittsburg to Chicago, known as the Pittsburg, Fort Wayne & Chicago Railroad, and was built by that company. It also owned the entire stock of a railway leading from Pittsburg, known as the Pittsburg, Cincinnati & St. Louis, which among its other lines had a line from Pittsburg to a point known as Bradford Junction, in the state of Indiana, I think it was, where it connected with a line which itself leased, known as the Chicago, St. Louis & Pittsburg, or at least at some time known by that name, which extended from Bradford Junction to Chicago; and the entire stock of the Pittsburg, Cincinnati & St. Louis Road was owned by the Pennsylvania Railroad Company. In 1870 the Pennsylvania Railroad Company caused to be incorporated in the state of Pennsylvania a holding and operating company, known as the Pennsylvania Company, to which it transferred its leases and its holding of stock in the lines west of Pittsburg. At the time of the organization of the Pennsylvania Company and the transfer to it by the Pennsylvania Railroad Company of its leases and stock holdings west of Pittsburg, the Pennsylvania Railroad Company, in consideration of such transfer, acquired and has ever since held the entire capital stock of the holding and operating company,—the Pennsylvania Company.

"Now, all of those are matters which existed at the time of the passage of the Act of 1890. And since then the Boston & Maine Railroad has gone on with the same policy of leasing and acquiring stock of parallel and competing lines, including the Boston & Lowell, with its connections—the Concord & Montreal, the Northern Railroad of New Hampshire, the

Central Railroad of Vermont, the Connecticut & Passumpsic, the Fitchburg Railroad, with its lessor—the Vermont & Massachusetts, and other lines—the result of which is that the Boston & Maine has acquired at least four of what were originally parallel and competing lines between the cities of Boston and Montreal and Quebec, and also at least two parallel and competing lines between Boston and the West, and still holds and operates them. And in like manner, the New York and New Haven Railroad Company, originally chartered to build and which did build a road from New York to New Haven of ninety miles—and the only road which it ever built, afterwards became consolidated with the New Haven, Hartford and Springfield Railroad Company, under the name it has ever since borne, the New York, New Haven & Hartford Road; and it has by a series of similar leases, acquisitions of stock, or purchases outright from other railroad companies, acquired a series of competing lines between Boston and New York—all rail lines, and lines of rail and water transportation, so that in point of fact a person cannot go by anything like a direct road from Boston to New York without going over one or the other of the roads which were originally parallel and competing, but which have been acquired in one of the different ways before stated by the New York, New Haven & Hartford Railroad Company. Among other acquisitions of the New York, New Haven & Hartford, they acquired a majority of or substantially all the stock of the New York and New England road—a parallel line which controlled one line of transportation on Long Island Sound (that from Norwich to New York); and by their acquisition of the Old Colony Railroad, through substantially a perpetual lease, and the ownership of a very large portion of its stock, secured a controlling interest in the Old Colony Steamship Company, and also the stock of the steamers running from Providence and Stonington to New York.

"Now, coming to the state of New York, we find that the New York Central and Hudson River road has also acquired the Rome, Watertown & Ogdensburg road by substantially a perpetual lease—which with its connections had been a direct competitor and rival of that company. And within a very few years the New York Central Company has acquired ninety-five per cent of the stock of the Lake Shore & Michigan Southern Company, and substantially the same amount of the stock of the Michigan Central Railroad Company, which, with its lessor company, the Canada Southern Company, operates a line from Buffalo to Chicago, being naturally and originally a competing line both with the Lake Shore & Michigan Southern and the Nickel Plate. So we have from New York City to Chicago, the New York Central controlling by stock ownership this series of roads which were its natural competitors.

"And so in the case of the Pennsylvania Railroad. Within a very short time, I think in the year 1899 or 1900, it acquired a controlling interest in the Baltimore & Ohio. The Pennsylvania road for many years had owned substantially all the stock of the Philadelphia, Wilmington & Baltimore Railroad Company, whose line extended from Philadelphia to Baltimore; and of the Baltimore and Potomac Railroad Company, whose line extended from Baltimore to Washington; and it operated these lines, and these lines from New York and Philadelphia made a through line from New York to Washington. The Baltimore & Ohio Railroad Company has owned a line for many years from Baltimore to Washington, and has operated other railroads for some years past, making a through line from New York to Washington and beyond Washington. And in the west and southwest the Baltimore & Ohio Railroad Company has had a line which touches all the principal points reached by the Pennsylvania Railroad, and competes with the Pennsylvania at Pittsburg, Cleveland, Sandusky, Wheeling, Chicago, Louisville and St. Louis, to say nothing of other points. The Chesapeake & Ohio Railroad Company has also been very much in the same position in regard to the Pennsylvania Railroad as the Baltimore & Ohio has been. The same is true to some extent of the Norfolk & Western Railroad. And within the last three years, I think it is, the Pennsylvania Railroad Company has acquired, if not a majority, at least very near that amount of the capital stock of each one of these railroads operating parallel and competing lines. So today no official of the government can go in or out of the city of Washington without riding over a railroad which is operated and controlled by some other railroad company also having parallel and competing lines going to the same place. That is true today and has been for some years.

"Now, we say that many of these matters have been necessarily well known, during all this period, to all the officers of the government, both before and since the passage of the Anti-trust Act. And they were done under the authority of state legislation which is plainly unconstitutional if these acts are restraints upon interstate commerce. Consequently we say that all of these matters are to be taken into consideration in determining, first, what congress intended by the passage of the act; and secondly, what the universal construction of the act has been since that time."

From the point of view of history, the Northern Securities Company is the logical culmination of a long series of events as old as the railway itself, in which the inherent tendencies toward combination have been in perpetual conflict with laws assuming natural competition. In this conflict the forms of co-operative effort and combination have been metamorphosed into new shapes to avoid the ban which the law had placed upon the old. These new forms have generally been slightly in advance of the law.

The lines of attack pursued by the government are indicated in the following series of propositions which, the assistant attorney general stated, had been derived from applicable decisions of the federal appellate courts, and which he applied to the facts of the merger under consideration:

1. Public policy requires free competition between competing transportation lines and forbids all attempts to restrict such competition or create a monopoly.

2. The police power extends to corporations which are engaged in a public service, and which are, therefore, subject to legislative control so far as becomes necessary for the protection of the public interests, and it is competent for the legislature of a state with respect to domestic trade, and congress with respect to interstate trade, to prohibit either corporations or individuals from combining, either directly or indirectly, so as to eliminate competition.

3. The purchase of stock by a railroad corporation in a competing line is contrary to public policy and void, and this

even though accomplished by individual stockholders, acting in behalf and for the interests of the purchasing company.

4. Where the direct and necessary result of a given combination is to eliminate competition, and thereby restrain trade, the intent to accomplish that result will be presumed and need not be formally proved.

5. It is not important that the proposed combination does not secure a complete monopoly of a given subject of commerce; a partial monopoly is equally offensive to public policy.

6. The fact that the power of the combination has not been exercised to increase prices or rates is not important. The law is concerned not with what is done, but with the power to do.

7. The law will look to the substance and not to the form, and will not permit a monopolistic combination, no matter by what corporate or legal devices it may be attempted.

8. Corporations as personalities only exist in a fiction of the law and for practical and beneficial purposes which subserve public interests. Where such fiction is evoked to violate criminal statutes or to defeat sound public policy, such fiction will be disregarded and the law will look to the acts of the individuals who control the corporation as the acts of the corporation itself.

9. Therefore, the mere fact that such a consolidation takes the form of a purchase by the stockholders of one company individually of a portion of the capital stock of a competing line will not legalize the transaction, and this notwithstanding the fact that the capital stock so purchased is less than a majority, provided it be purchased with a view to the control of the competing line.

10. The liberty guaranteed by the fifth amendment to purchase and sell property is clearly subject to the police power of the state, and does not sanction purchases and sales of capital stock with a view to a practical consolidation of parallel and competing lines.

CHAPTER VI.

DECISIONS OF THE FEDERAL TRIAL COURT AND OF THE UNITED STATES CIRCUIT COURT.

Two different decisions were rendered in this case by circuit judges of the United States before it reached the supreme court for the first time. The one by four judges,[26] referred to above, sitting as a trial court, under a special act of congress; the other by the regular circuit court.[27] The former decided the case brought by the federal government, and the latter that brought by the state of Minnesota.

The decision of the trial court, written by Judge Thayer and concurred in by the other three, recites very briefly the facts derived "from admissions made by the pleadings as well as from much oral testimony." Subsequent to the acquisition of the Burlington, recites the court, certain influential stockholders of the Great Northern and Northern Pacific, "acting in concert with each other," placed the great majority of the stock of the two constituent companies in the hands of a single person, the Securities Company. This destroyed every motive for competition between natural competitors. Since every person "is presumed to intend what is the necessary consequence of his own acts, when done willfully and deliberately, we must conclude that those who conceived and executed" this plan intended to restrain commerce and acquire the power of establishing unreasonable rates. The fact that unreasonable rates have not yet been established is no guarantee against extortion in the future, for the power to extort exists in the hands of the Security Company. This is prohibited by the Anti-trust act, which declares illegal every combination in the

---

[26] Circuit Judges; Caldwell, Sanborn, Thayer, Van Devanter.
[27] Circuit Judge; Lochren.

form of a trust or *otherwise*. The generality of the language
of the act indicates the desire of congress to prohibit every
scheme which might be devised to restrain trade, whether
known at the time of enactment or whether still to be invented.
The Securities Company accomplishes the object which congress has declared illegal perhaps more effectually than other
forms of combination generally known in 1890 when the Anti-
trust law was passed. Nor would the prohibition of an arrangement like the Securities Company constitute an undue,
perhaps unconstitutional, restriction of the right of private
property and of private contracts, for congress has the power,
under the constitution, to prevent a citizen from entering "into
those private contracts which directly and substantially, or indirectly, remotely, incidentally and collaterally" restrain commerce among the states. Referring to the contention of the
defendants that since the Securities Company had been fully
organized and the majority of the stock of the two railways
acquired before the bill of the government was filed no relief
could be granted to the government, the court held that "it
would be a novel, not to say absurd, interpretation of the Anti-
trust act to hold that after an unlawful combination is formed
and has acquired the power which it had no right to acquire
. . . and is proceeding to use it and execute the purpose for which the combination was formed, it must be left in
possession of the power that it has acquired, with full freedom
to exercise it." One of the objects for which the Securities
Company was formed was the promotion of commerce. Upon
this point the court expressed itself as follows:

"It may be that such a virtual consolidation of parallel and
competing lines of railroad as has been effected, taking a broad
view of the situation, is beneficial to the public rather than
harmful.

"It may be that the motives which inspired the combination
by which this end was accomplished were wholly laudable and
unselfish; that the combination was formed by the individual
defendants to protect great interests which had been committed to their charge; or that the combination was the initial
and the necessary step in the accomplishment of great designs,
which, if carried out as they were conceived, would prove to

be of inestimable value to the communities which these roads
serve and to the country at large.

"We shall neither affirm nor deny either of these propositions, because they present issues which we are not called
upon to determine, and some of them involve questions which
are not within the province of any court to decide, involving,
as they do, questions of public policy which congress must determine.

"It is our duty to ascertain whether the proof discloses a
combination in direct restraint of interstate commerce,—that
is to say, a combination whereby the power has been acquired
to suppress competition between two or more competing and
parallel lines of railroad engaged in interstate commerce.

"If it does disclose such a combination, and we have little
hesitation in answering this question in the affirmative, then
the anti-trust act, as it has been heretofore interpreted by the
court of last resort, has been violated and the government is
entitled to a decree."

In accordance with these conclusions the court declared the
acquisition of the stock by the Securities Company, illegal;
it enjoined the Securities Company from acquiring additional
stock, from voting the stock already acquired, and from paying
dividends on its stock or exercising any control whatsoever
over the corporate acts of the Great Northern and Northern
Pacific Railway Companies. Permission to return to share-
holders the stock not held was expressly granted. So much
of the decree of this court as restrains the two railway companies from paying over to the Securities Company dividends
upon shares owned by it was subsequently suspended by the
court during the appeal of the case to the supreme court on
condition that the litigation would be prosecuted with due
diligence.

The difference between the opinion of the trial court in the
federal case just described and the opinion of the United States
Circuit Court in the state case are clearly fore-shadowed in the
statement of facts in the latter opinion. Judge Lochren states
briefly the facts of organization of the Great Northern and
Northern Pacific railway companies; he refers to the interests
of the state of Minnesota as a land owner, shipper, and pur-

chaser of supplies; he summarizes the legal facts of the state anti-consolidation and anti-trust acts; he presents the substance of Hill's testimony in regard to the importance of back-loading and the economic and strategic value of the Burlington; he passes in brief review the conflict in the stock market between the Union Pacific and the Northern Pacific interests, which culminated in the formation of a holding company, with which neither the Great Northern Company nor the Northern Pacific Company had anything to do; and finally, he accepts "as the purpose and intent" on the part of the promoters of the Securities Company their desire to secure the Northern Pacific Company against the danger of any future raid upon its stock which might place its management and the resulting control of the Burlington system in the power of any rival railroad corporation whose interests might be hostile to the development of the property of the Northern Pacific and Great Northern companies and their seaboard terminals, and of the region of country traversed by their railroad systems. It is his opinion that "the evidence fails to show that the Securities Company was formed for the purpose of acquiring and holding a majority of the stock of the Great Northern Company as well as that of the Northern Pacific Company, although that result followed soon after, and may have been desired and anticipated." The Trans-Missouri, Joint Traffic Addyston Pipe, Pearsall and other leading cases, considered also by the trial court and figuring greatly in all the briefs, lead Judge Lochren to deduce the general proposition "that contracts which do not directly and necessarily affect transportation or rates therefor, are not in restraint of trade or within the statute (State Anti-trust Act), even though they may remotely and indirectly appear to have some probable effect in that direction." The Securites Company, unlike the Trans-Missouri Freight Association and analogous organizations, is merely an investor in and owner of shares of railway stock. It is not a railway company. Its franchise confers no power to manage railways with respect to rates. "There is no scintilla of evidence that it has sought to control or interfere in respect to any of these matters." In short, the formation of the Securities Company involved no act or contract in restraint of trade or commerce or affecting transportation rates, more than any ordinary transfer of railroad stock from one person to another. "The formation of the Northern Securities Company and its holdings of stock has and can have nothing to do directly or indirectly with trade, commerce, transportation or rates." It is regarded unjust to presume that the Great Northern and Northern Pacific companies will contract illegally with each other for the control of rates and in restraint of trade; if so, they will "for the first time" violate the anti-trust act of Minnesota, and the corporations and their offending officials will be amenable to punishment, and to appropriate legal or equitable proceedings." The decision rejects the doctrine that the mere possession of power warrants an assumption of the criminal use of such power.

The vital point of difference in the two opinions is admirably summarized in a private letter,[28] a part of which is here inserted:

"The state case and the government case are identical as respects the construction to be given to the 'Sherman Anti-trust Act.' The circuit judges decided that the purchase of a majority of shares by a single interest was criminal because of the voting power of the shares and the necessary inference that the power would be exercised to restrain competition. Judge Lochren holds directly the reverse.

"Let me give you an illustration to make the point of difference clear: A ferry company, organized in Minnesota with a capital of $100,000.00, is operating a ferry-boat between Duluth, in Minnesota, and Superior, in Wisconsin. A Wisconsin company with the same capital is operating a competing ferry-boat between the same points. A person or corporation purchases a majority of the shares of each company. The circuit judges decided that such a purchase, being in direct restraint of competition, is criminal. Judge Lochren holds the reverse."

The following parallel readings will afford additional comparisons between the two decisions:

---

[28] M. D. Grover, General Counsel for the Great Northern Ry. Co.

OFINION OF TRIAL COURT.

(1) According to the familiar rule that every one is presumed to intend what is the necessary consequence of his own acts, when done willfully and deliberately, we must conclude that those who conceived and executed the plan aforesaid intended, among other things, to accomplish these objects.

(2) To this end, these stockholders arranged and agreed with each other to procure and cause the formation of a corporation under the laws of the State of New Jersey, which latter company, when organized, should buy all or at least the greater part of the stock of the Northern Pacific and Great Northern Companies.

(3) It confers the power to establish unreasonable rates and directly restrains commerce by placing obstacles in the way of free and unrestricted competition between carriers who are natural rivals for patronage.

(4) Competition, we think, would not be more effectually restrained than it now is under and by force of the existing arrangement, if the two railroad companies were con-

OPINION OF CIRCUIT COURT.

(1) I am compelled to reject the doctrine that any person can be held to have committed, or to be purposing and about to commit a highly penal offense, merely because it can be shown that his pecuniary interests will be thereby advanced, and that he has the power, either directly by himself, or indirectly through persuasion or coercion of his agents, to compass the commission of the offense.

(2) The evidence therefore fails to show that the Northern Securities Company was formed for the purpose of acquiring and holding a majority of the stock of the Great Northern Company as well as that of the Northern Pacific Company.

(3) It is not a railroad company and has no franchise or power to manage or operate or direct the management or operation of either railroad in respect to rates or charges for transportation, or otherwise.

(4) The decision of the case last cited, (i. e. Trial Court) as I read it and understand it, does not specify or point out any contract,

solidated under a single charter.

(5) It is almost too plain for argument that the defendants would have violated the Anti-trust Act if they had done, through the agency of natural persons, what they have accomplished through an artificial person of their own creation. . . . .

What has been done through the organization of the Securities Company accomplishes the object, which congress has denounced as illegal, more effectually, perhaps, than such a combination as is last supposed. . . .

It will not do to say that so long as each railroad company has its own board of directors they operate independently and are not controlled by the owner of the majority of their stock. It is the common experience of mankind that the acts of corporations are dictated and that their policy is controlled by those who own the majority of their stock.

agreement or act on the part of the defendants, or of any of them, which is directly in restraint of trade or commerce, or which has any direct reference to trade, commerce, transportation or rates; nor even any threat or avowed purpose on the part of any defendant to do any such act, or enter into any such contract or agreement.

(5) The case is far from sustaining the idea that if a single investor in railroad stocks, whether a natural person or a corporation without railroad franchises, should acquire, by purchase, a majority or the whole of the stock of both the Northern Pacific Company and the Great Northern Company, that would work any consolidation of those two companies, or that such purchaser would have any power to manage or operate the railroads of both or either of said railroad companies.

CHAPTER VII.

FIRST DECISION OF THE UNITED STATES SU-PREME COURT.

In addition to the decision of the majority of the court, two dissenting and one concurring opinion must be considered. The majority decision, which was written by Justice Harlan, opens with the text of the Sherman Anti-Trust Law of 1890, followed by a consideration of the questions whether or not a combination or conspiracy in restraint of trade or commerce among the states or with foreign states has been shown by the pleadings and the evidence, and whether or not the case is one in which the defendants may be properly chargeable with monopolizing or attempting to monopolize any part of such trade or commerce. The court then recites briefly the facts leading up to the organization of the Northern Securities Company, endorsing in this connection[29] that part of the decision of the trial court which characterized the Northern Securities arrangement as one by which the control of the Great Northern and Northern Pacific Railways was vested in a "common body, to wit the holding corporation, with not only the power but the duty to pursue a policy which would promote the interests" of both systems of railways at the expense of the public and removing all inducements for competition between them. Within the meaning of the Anti-Trust Act this arrangement is characterized as a combination in restraint of interstate and international commerce, which alone is sufficient to bring it under the condemnation of the law.[30] The court holds that if the Anti-Trust Act does not

---

[29] Decision (193 U. S. 197) : 2-4. The paging adopted in this monograph is the paging of the edition of the decisions issued by the Department of Justice.

[30] Ibid : 11.

5

embrace the Northern Securities arrangement, the plain intention of the legislative branch of the government will be defeated. "If congress has not, by the words used in the Act, described this and like cases, it would, we apprehend, be impossible to find words that would describe them."[31] The court recognizes as valid the charges of the government that if the combination was held to be not in violation of the act of congress, "then the efforts of the national government to preserve to the people the benefits of free competition among carriers engaged in interstate commerce will be wholly unavailing, and all transcontinental lines, indeed the entire railway systems of the country, may be absorbed, merged and consolidated, thus placing the public at the absolute mercy of the holding corporation."[32] The holding corporation would cause all constituent companies to cease actively to compete for trade and commerce along their respective lines, and make them one powerful consolidated corporation. Stock-holders of the holding company are interested primarily in preventing all competition between the constituent lines, and as owners of stock or of certificates of stock in the holding company, they will see to it that no competition is tolerated.[33] Whether the free operation of the normal laws of competition is a wise and wholesome rule for trade and commerce is an economic question which the court is not called upon to consider or to determine.[34] Congress has the power under the constitution to establish rules by which interstate and international commerce shall be governed. It has prescribed as one such rule the rule of free competition among those engaged in such commerce, and the "natural effect of competition is to increase commerce." Any constitutional guarantee of the liberty of contract does not prevent congress from prescribing the rule of free competition for those engaged in interstate and international commerce.[35] Earlier decisions of the court have held that liberty of contract does not involve the right to deprive the public of the advantages of free competition in trade

[31] U. S. S. C. (193 U. S. 197) : 31.
[32] Ibid: 6.
[33] Ibid: 7.
[34] Ibid: 15.
[35] Ibid: 11.

and commerce. Liberty of contract does not imply liberty
in a corporation or individuals to defy the national will when
legally expressed. Nor does the enforcement of the legal
enactment of congress infringe in any proper sense the general inherent right of every one to acquire and hold property.
That right, like all other rights, must be exercised in subordi-
nation to the law.[36] It will be recalled that the argument
with respect to the free exercise of the rights of property was
strongly emphasized before the trial court, and in substance
it was repeated before the supreme court. "I do not deny the
very spirited contention that the construction we put upon the
law in question interferes with the power of people to do what
they will with their property. That was the very object of
the law, and it was certainly contemplated that the rights of
purchase, sale and contract would be controlled so far as necessary to prevent these rights from being exercised to defeat the
law."[37] Many students of economics will probably ask the
question, why this particular point did not receive more at-
tention at the hands of the court. The court expressed the
opinion that if the certificate of incorporation of the Securities
Company had expressly stated that the object of the company
was to destroy competition between competing parallel lines
of interstate carriers, all would have seen at the outset that
the scheme was in hostility to the national government, and
that there was a purpose to violate or evade the act of congress. It is also asserted that nothing in the record tends to
show that the state of New Jersey had any reason to suspect
that those who took advantage of its liberal incorporation laws
had in view, when organizing the Securities Company, the
destruction of competition between two great railway carriers
engaged in interstate commerce in distant states of the
union.[38] With reference to the argument that railway corporations created under the laws of the state can only be consolidated with the authority of the state, the court holds that
even if the state allowed consolidations, it would not follow
that the stockholders of two or more state railway corpora-

---

[36] U. S. S. C. (193 U. S. 197) : 25.
[37] Oral argument of the Attorney General of The United States, 29: 69.
[38] U. S. S. C. (193 U. S. 197) : 20.

tions, having competing lines and engaged in interstate commerce, could lawfully combine to form a distinct corporation to hold the stock of the constituent corporations, and by destroying competition between them, in violation of the act of congress, restrain commerce among the states and with foreign nations.[39] Generally speaking, the supreme court follows the main lines of thought represented by the decision of the trial court and expressly states that the "circuit court has done only what the actual situation demanded." The decree, if executed, will destroy, not the property interests of the original stockholders of the constituent companies, but the power of the holding corporation as the instrument of the illegal combination. In affirming the judgment of the court below, and giving permission to this court to proceed in the execution of its decree, as the circumstances may require, the United States supreme court put an end to that type of holding corporations which is created with the distinct purpose of acquiring and holding shares of stock of parallel and competing lines.

The concurring opinion of Justice Brewer is in some respects the most noteworthy feature of the decision, because Justice Brewer indicates a way out of the difficulties into which the construction placed upon the Anti-Trust law by the court will inevitably lead. He cannot assent to all that is stated in the opinion of the court. In some respects the reasons given for the judgments in the Trans-Missouri, Joint Traffic, and similar cases referred to by him, cannot be sustained. Instead of holding that the Anti-Trust Act includes all contracts, reasonable or unreasonable, in restraint of interstate trade, Justice Brewer holds that the ruling should have been that the contracts presented in the Joint Traffic and similar cases were unreasonable restraints of interstate trade, and as such they fell within the scope of the law. The Anti-Trust Act was leveled only at unlawful restraints and monopolies. Congress did not intend to reach and destroy those minor contracts in partial restraint of trade which that long course of decisions in common law had affirmed were reasonable and ought to be upheld. Most economists will welcome this dis-

---

[39] U. S. S. C. (193 U. S. 197) : 15.

tinction between reasonable and unreasonable restraints of
trade, but it may not be obvious to all how this position, although accurate in their estimation, can be reconciled with
an earlier statement in Justice Brewer's opinion, that the
Trans-Missouri and Joint Traffic "cases were rightly decided."[40] Another important point in Justice Brewer's decision relates to the right of the individual to manage his own
property and determine the place and manner of its investment. Freedom of action in these respects is among the inalienable rights of every citizen. In applying this law to the
present case, it appeared that Mr. Hill was the owner of the
majority of the stock in the Great Northern Railway Company, and he could not by any act of Congress be deprived of
the right of investing his surplus means in the purchase of
stock of the Northern Pacific Railway Company, although
such purchase might tend to vest in him, through that ownership, a control over both companies. In other words, the
right which all other citizens had of purchasing Northern
Pacific stock could not be denied to him by congress because
of his ownership of stock in the Great Northern Company.[41]
A corporation is not endowed with the inalienable rights of a
natural person. The Securities Company was a mere instrumentality by which separate railway properties were combined
under one control. A holding corporation of this type would
make it possible, by means of a series of progressive consolidations, to vest the control of all the railway properties of the
United States in single hands. Justice Brewer does not en-
large upon the alleged beneficence of free and unrestricted
competition among railways. He recognizes that a single
railway is, if not a legal, largely a practical monopoly, and that
a holding company may extend and broaden such monopoly. In
conclusion, Justice Brewer says that he felt constrained to
make these observations for fear that the broad and sweeping
language of the opinion of the court might tend to unsettle
legitimate business enterprises, stifle or retard wholesome
business activity and encourage improper disregard of reasonable contract, and invite unnecessary litigation.

---

[40] Ibid: 33.
[41] Ibid: 34.

The dissenting opinion, written by Justice White and concurred in by the Chief Justice and Justices Peckham and Holmes, is devoted chiefly to the consideration of two questions: First, does the Anti-Trust Act, when rightly interpreted, apply to the acquisition and ownership by the Northern Securities Company of the stock in the two railroads; and second, if it does, had congress the power to regulate or control such acquisition and ownership? At the root of the case lies the question of power, and the case for the government depends upon the proposition that the ownership of stock in railway corporations created by a state is interstate commerce wherever the railway is engaged in interstate commerce.[42] It should be noted, too, that this opinion concedes at the outset that the Northern Pacific and the Great Northern are "in some aspects" competing railways. Obviously an answer to the question whether or not the acquisition and ownership of the railway shares in question is interstate commerce depends upon the accepted definition of interstate commerce. Such a definition, and one which has been accepted many times by the court, is found in Gibbons vs. Ogden and reads as follows: "Commerce undoubtedly is traffic, but it is something more, it is intercourse; it describes the commercial intercourse between nations and parts of nations in all its branches, and is regulated by prescribing rules for carrying on that intercourse."[43] If the commerce clause of the constitution authorizes congress to regulate the ownership of the stock in railways chartered by state authority, the tenth amendment will have been destroyed and practically no powers left to the states exclusively, in case it can be shown that any of these powers have reference to the ownership of property which in the most indirect manner can be associated with interstate commerce. It would give congress the right to abrogate every railway charter granted by the states, if congress deemed that the rights conferred by such state charters tended to restrain commerce between the states or to create a monopoly concerning such commerce. It would give congress the power to dissolve consolidations expressly authorized by the laws

---

[42] U. S. S. C. (193 U. S. 197): 39.
[43] Ibid: 40.

of the several states or to permit consolidations expressly prohibited by state laws. The principle that the ownership of property is embraced within the power of congress to regulate commerce violates the most elementary conceptions of the rights of property; for it would follow that if congress considered the acquisition by one or more individuals engaged in interstate commerce of more than a certain amount of property would be prejudicial to interstate commerce, the amount of property held or the amount which could be employed in interstate commerce could be regulated.[44] Justice White states that his mind fails to seize the distinction that the right of the Securities Company to hold this stock is one thing and the power of individuals or corporations when not organized for the purpose of holding this stock is an entirely different thing. Similar ownership of the same property by one or more individuals is involved, and the same alleged restraint or monopoly and prohibition of this holding under the law must be a necessary consequence. The suggested distinction is to him an incongruity which would do violence to both the letter and the spirit of the constitution, since it would in effect hold that although a particular act was a burden upon interstate commerce or a monopoly thereof, individuals could lawfully do the act, provided only that they did not use the instrumentality of a holding corporation.[45] The decree of the lower court, while it forbids the use of the stock of the Northern Securities Company, authorizes its return to the alleged conspirators and does not restrain them from exercising the control resulting from the ownership. "If the conspiracy and combination existed and was illegal, my mind fails to perceive why it should be left to produce its full force and effect in the hands of individuals by whom it was charged the conspiracy was entered into."[46] Reference is made to the consolidations represented by the Boston & Maine, New York, New Haven and Hartford, New York Central, the Pennsylvania, and other railway systems, and the conclusion is drawn that since congress had full knowledge of these facts at the time of the

[44] Ibid: 42.
[45] Ibid: 43.
[46] Ibid: 43.

enactment of the Anti-Trust Law in 1890, it must have been universally understood by members of congress that the authority to regulate these organizations lay with the states, and that the states and not congress had control of the subject-matter of the organization and ownership of railways created by the states.[47] The Northern Securities is the first case in which this power of congress has been asserted. Justice White refers to the Joint Traffic and Trans-Missouri cases, not because they are apposite to the Northern Securities case, "for they are not, since the contracts which were involved in them vitally concerned interstate commerce, while in this case the sole question is whether the ownership of stock in competing railroads itself involved interstate commerce." He refers to these cases because they illustrate the distinction which the supreme court has always maintained between the power of congress over interstate commerce and its want of authority to regulate subjects not embraced within that grant.[48] A number of other cases are similarly referred to for the purpose of showing that in the light of these decisions the ownership of stock of competing railways is not interstate commerce. Referring to the contention that the power of congress over interstate commerce includes the authority to regulate the instruments of such commerce, Judge White holds that the power to regulate instrumentalities is entirely distinct from the power to regulate the acquisition and ownership of such instrumentalities.[49] A position very similar to that assumed by Judge Lochren is maintained in the present opinion when it is asserted that "to maintain the contention, therefore, it must be decided that because ownership of property if acquired may be so used as to burden commerce, therefore to acquire and own is a burden."[50] In other words, Justice White believes that the majority opinion confuses the two ideas of the ownership and the use of property, and holds that the right of the government to control the use of property affords no foundation for the proposition that there exists in government a power to limit the quantity and character of

[47] U. S. S. C. (193 U. S. 197): 45.
[48] Ibid: 53.
[49] Ibid: 57.
[50] Ibid: 59.

property which may be acquired and owned. The difference between the two is the difference between a free and constitutional government restrained by law and an absolute government unrestrained by any of the principles which are necessary in the perpetuation of society and the protection of life, liberty and property.

Great cases, like hard cases, make bad law, says Justice Holmes in his individual opinion; for great cases are called great not by reason of their real importance in shaping the law of the future, but because of some accident of immediate overwhelming interest which appeals to the feelings and distorts the judgment.[51] It is by no means difficult to receive the suggestion of the influence of immediate overwhelming interest in shaping the views of the majority of the court. Justice Holmes holds that the Anti-Trust Act is a criminal statute, and that it is vain to insist that this is not a criminal proceeding. "The words cannot be read one way in a suit which is to end in fine and in imprisonment and in another way in one which seeks an injunction." In consideration of the position assumed in the majority opinion, he holds that whatever is criminal when done by way of combination is equally criminal if done by a single man. The position of the government depends upon the effect which the purchase of the shares of stock may have upon the competitive relations of the two railways. "If such a remote result of the exercise to an ordinary extent of property and personal freedom is enough to make the exercise unlawful, there is hardly any transaction concerning commerce between the states that may not be made a crime by the finding of jury or court. The personal ascendancy of one man may be such that it will give to his advice the effect of a command, if he own but a single share in each road. The tendency of his presence in the stockholders' meeting may be certain to prevent competition, and thus his advice, if not his mere existence, become a crime."[52] We may add to this the words of Justice White to the effect that "the doctrine must in reason lead to the concession of the right in congress to regulate concerning the

---

[51] Ibid : 63.
[52] Ibid : 65

aptitude, the character, and the capacity of persons."[53]   The
Anti-Trust law hits two classes of cases, and only two: contracts in restraint of trade and combinations or conspiracies
in restraint of trade,[54] and the existence of neither of these
has been proved by the evidence and pleadings.   In his opinion there is no attempt to monopolize and no combination in
restraint of trade until something is done with the intent to
exclude strangers to the combination from competing with it
in some part of the business which it carries on.   The Anti-
Trust law says nothing about competition and only prevents
its suppression by contracts or combinations in restraint of
trade.   Justice Holmes closes his opinion in the following
words: "I am happy to know that only a minority of my
brethren adopted an interpretation of the law which in my
opinion would make eternal the *bellum omnium contra omnes*,
and disintegrate society so far as it could into individual atoms.
If that were its intent, I should regard calling such a law a
regulation of commerce as a mere pretence.   It would be an
attempt to reconstruct society.   I am not concerned with the
wisdom of such an attempt, but I believe that congress was
not entrusted by the constitution with the power of making it,
and I am deeply persuaded that it has not tried."[55]

The four decisions which have just been discussed were
rendered on March 14, 1904.   On April 11, the supreme court
rendered the decision on the appeal from the decision of Judge
Lochren, discussed in detail in Chapter V.   The supreme court
holds that it is without jurisdiction, and the case is sent back
with directions that it be remanded to the state court.   The
state of Minnesota, as was noted above, had brought suit in
the state courts, and on petition of the Northern Securities
Company the case was transferred to the United States circuit court on the ground that violations of both the state laws
and the federal anti-trust laws were involved.   Considerable
controversy arose over the right to remove the case to the federal court, with the result that the Unted States circuit court
assumed jurisdiction which has now been declared by the

---

[53] U. S. S. C. (193 U. S. 197): 60.
[54] Ibid: 65.
[55] Ibid: 70.

supreme court to have been unwarranted. Commenting on the contention, of the state that it had proprietary interests in the case, the court said: "The injury on account of which the present suit was brought is at most only remote and indirect. . . . . If Minnesota may, by an original suit in its name, invoke the jurisdiction of the circuit court, because alone of the alleged remote and indirect injury to its proprietary interests arising from the mere absence of free competition in trade and commerce as carried on by interstate carriers within its limits, then every state, upon like grounds, may maintain, in its name, in the circuit court of the United States, a suit against interstate carriers engaged in business within their respective limits." The supreme court remanded the case to the state court in the following language: "For the reasons stated, we are of the opinion that the suit does not—to use the words of the act of 1875—really and substantially involve a dispute or controversy within the jurisdiction of the circuit court for the purpose of the final decree. That being the case, the circuit court following the mandate of the statute, should not have proceeded therein, but should have remanded the cause to the state court." The decision of the supreme court, consequently, leaves the case of the state of Minnesota against the Northern Securities Company at this date[56] in exactly the same condition that it was before the United States government instituted its proceedings.

---

[56] March, 1904. Nothing has been done with it since.

CHAPTER VIII.

EVENTS FOLLOWING THE FIRST DECISION OF THE SUPREME COURT.

Soon after the supreme court decision, March 22, President Hill[57] issued a circular to the share-holders of the Northern Securities Company announcing a resolution of the Board of Directors, which was adopted with a view to meeting the decree of the court. The circular briefly refers to the beneficial effects which, in his estimation, the company has wrought by increasing commerce and reducing rates; it states that in the organization of the company no commissions were paid nor was any other expense incurred, except what was necessary in obtaining the charter and for the economical conduct of the affairs of the company; that the acquisition of the stock of the Northern Pacific and the Great Northern was made in the full belief that such purchase was not in violation of any law of the United States, which opinion, says the circular, has been approved by four justices of the United States supreme court; and that, in view of the adverse decision of the court, it was necessary to reduce the capital stock of the company and distribute to its share-holders the shares of the two constituent companies. The opinion was expressed that the order of the court would be fully and promptly complied with. A stockholders' meeting was announced for April 21 at the company's office in Hoboken, N. J., and the transfer books for purposes of this meeting were to be closed on April 18, 1904. Under the laws of New Jersey a two-thirds vote of the share-holders is necessary in order to reduce the capital stock. In order to make it possible to distribute the May and subsequent dividends, prompt action was declared to be necessary. The prop-

---

[57] See copy of circular, appendix 7.

osition to be voted on provided in substance a reduction of the capital stock of the Northern Securities Company from 3,954,000 shares to 39,540 shares. The 99 per cent. of the present outstanding shares were to be called in for surrender and cancellation, and against each share of the stock thus surrendered the Securities Company was to deliver $39.27 stock of the Northern Pacific Railway Company, and $30.17 stock of the Great Northern Railway Company, and proportionate amounts for each fraction of a share of stock surrendered.

There were present at the stockholders' meeting of April 21, either in person or by proxy, 1,829 stockholders or about 72.75 per cent of the total number. This number of stockholders held 2,944,740 shares of the stock of the Securities Company or about 74½ per cent of the total outstanding capital stock. Excluding the 824,918 shares held by the Harriman interests there were absent from the stockholders' meeting less than 5 per cent of the total stock of the company. All the shares present at the meeting voted in favor of the plan proposed in the circular of March 22,[58] 1904. The Harriman interests protested at once that the plan of distribution was illegal and in violation of their rights.[59]

On April 2, 1904, E. H. Harriman, Winslow S. Pierce, and the Oregon Short Line Railway Company petitioned the four circuit judges who had entered the original decree for leave to intervene with respect to the execution of this decree. The petitioners asserted that since November 18, 1901, they had been the registered owners and holders of $82,491,871 par value of the capital stock of the Northern Securities Company, that these shares had been held in trust by the Equitable Trust Company of New York for the petitioners, and that the execution of the decree of the court would, in their opinion, necessitate the restoration of the status quo of the fall of 1901. Other facts relating to the original acquisition of these shares were enumerated. The petitioners discussed the pro rata plan for the distribution of the Northern Securities stock, as proposed by the board of directors, which they believed to be inequitable and unjust, and they asserted that they were will-

[58] 39: 105. See also circular of June 11, 1904, Appendix S.
[59] 41: 16.

ing to restore to the Northern Securities Company the original certificates of stock held by them. They argued that the pro rata plan, if consummated, would vest a majority of the stock of both the Great Northern and the Northern Pacific Railway Companies in the same individual stock-holders of the Great Northern Company who originally co-operated in the promotion and organization of the Northern Securities Company and who were still co-operating and acting in concert and combination and would continue the common management and direction of the two competing railway companies, and thus render the decree of the court ineffectual and defeat or evade its true intent and purpose. In view of all these facts, the petitioners prayed the court to enjoin and restrain the Securities Company from distributing its present holdings of stock under the proposed plan of pro rata distribution. This petition was served not only upon the attorneys for the Northern Securities Company, but also upon the attorney general of the United States. When the matter came up for hearing the attorney general filed a statement, saying that he had received a copy of the petition, that he did not affirm or deny its allegations, that the case had proceeded to final judgment, and that he objected to the intervention. "Upon appeal by the defendants to the supreme court of the United States, the decree of this court was confirmed in every particular, the effect of which was to end and close the case. The United States stands on the decree as affirmed, and submits that the court is only concerned to see that it is faithfully observed by the defendants according to its terms."[60] The petition was heard at St. Louis, beginning March 12, before the circuit judges who composed the trial court.[61]

The real question at issue was the construction of the decree, the petitioners claiming that a ratable distribution was forbidden by the decree, and a return *in specie* was demanded. They assumed that the title of the railway shares never passed to the Securities Company, but that the court by its decree had ordered their return. They maintained that by the amendment of the suit the United States acquired constructive cus-

[60] Letter of Attorney General Knox.
[61] See p. 272.

tody of or domination over the railway shares acquired by the Northern securities Company, and that by the decree the company was required to return the railway shares it received to those originally transferring them or their assignees. The attorney general interposed no objection to the ratable distribution which the petitioners characterized as an evasion of the decree. The court was asked to make the present permissive direction mandatory, and to provide simply in the decree that in its execution a return *in specie* shall be made obligatory. One of the attorneys for Harriman pointed out to the court the great benefits which would follow the possession of the Northern Pacific, and through it the Burlington, by the Oregon Short Line and Union Pacific interests. "Under the statutes of Utah, the Oregon Short Line Railway Company has power to hold this Northern Pacific stock; under the laws of Utah the Union Pacific would have that power; under the laws of congress the Union Central has the power; under the laws of congress the Union Pacific would have the power to hold this stock, because at no two points served by these roads is there any competition, and the characterizing of competition for trans-continental business is entirely different."[62] Carrying out this idea, the same counsel maintained that if Harriman secured control over the Northern Pacific, he would promptly sever the connection between that railway and the Great Northern and Burlington. He claimed that Harriman could do much more for the Burlington than it was possible for Hill to do. "Where the Burlington gives to these two railways the markets of two or three states, the Union Pacific will give them access to the markets of thirteen states. Where this combination would give the Great Northern and the Northern Pacific access to one port, the combination of the Northern Pacific with the Union Pacific, through the Oregon Short line would give the people of the Northwest access to a dozen ports from San Francisco to New Orleans."[63] A list of states is then enumerated which will be served by the Union Pacific, if the "great plan conceived by the genius" of Harriman can be carried out. "The heavy freight of lumber or rough ma-

---

[62] Argument of Mr. W. D. Guthrie; also 32, 33.
[63] Argument of Mr. W. D. Guthrie.

terial which Mr. Hill describes in his testimony, and which he throws through the Burlington, cramped up as it is to the middle states, is to be sent down to the south and southwest, and over the rocky mountains, and scattered all over this country in ten-fold to the markets that the Burlington system can afford."[64]

The counsel for the Securities Company maintained that the decree of the court forbids action, but does not command it. It forbids the Northern Securities Company from voting or receiving dividends upon the railway shares, and the railway companies are forbidden from paying dividends on them to it. It was assumed that the concluding portion of the decree: "Nothing herein shall be construed to prohibit a return of the shares," was inserted to prevent any misapprehension of the provisions of the decree restraining voting power, that the court did not undertake to give any course or make any command with respect to the distribution of the shares, and that this matter was left entirely to the Securities Company, as the legal owner of the shares. It was further argued that if the Securities Company has legal title to the shares, it is its right and duty to distribute them pro rata among its share-holders. If it did not acquire legal title to them and the transaction was unlawful under the anti-trust law, Harriman was a party to an unlawful act, and having been a party to it, had no standing in equity. Harriman was a director of the Northern Pacific Railway Company, and a member of its executive committee. He was also a director of the Northern Securities Company, and a member of its executive committee. As a director he voted authorizing the sale of the shares to the Northern Securities Company for cash to the amount of millions of dollars. The shares of the Northern Pacific Railway Company have increased in value many millions of dollars. Under the petition, Harriman, in the Union Pacific interests, would not only get the Northern Pacific shares, but the increase in value, thus depriving other share-holders of the Security Company of any part of this increase. The relative status of the Harriman holdings of Northern Securities shares under the

---

[64] Argument of W. D. Guthrie.

proposed pro rata distribution and under the plan advocated by Mr. Harriman together with the income from each of these plans is shown below:

Character of Harriman holdings.	Par value of stock held,	Annual income.
Northern Sec. stock at 4 per cent. rate	$82,491,871	$3,299,674
Northern Sec. stock at 4¼ per cent. rate......................	82,491,871	3,712,134
Great Northern and Northern Pacific under pro rata distribution.......	56,709,330	3,969,667
Northern Pacific stock under original holdings, dividend rate 7 per cent.................	78,108,000	5,467,560

It was also argued that the petitioners were seeking gain through delay. "I do not doubt that he (the petitioner) would like to have blazoned through the newspapers of this country and Europe the announcement that your Honors had said that this distribution of the property shall be indefinitely postponed, and the result will be that if they fail in the evidence in getting the iniquitous demand that they make gratified in the award to them of the shares they claim, they will indirectly, through that delay, accomplish their purposes, by scaring from their holdings the very many people who could illy afford so to be dealt with, to make them sell their shares and pick them up at prices that will enable them then to have, if this court don't decree it, the majority that it wants.[65]

On April 19, 1904, the decision of the circuit judges was rendered. It denied unanimously the application of the petitioners upon the following grounds:

(1) The plan of the directors of the Northern Securities Company for the distribution of the stock of the Great Northern and Northern Pacific Railway Companies is not violative of the decree in the Northern Securities case.

(2) No one but the United States can successfully appeal to the court to enjoin the execution of that plan on the ground that it is in violation of the Sherman Anti-Trust act, and the United States expresses satisfaction with the present decree.

(3) The stock of the two railway companies is not in the custody of the court.

---

[65] John G. Johnson, Oral Argument.

6

(4)   An intervention is not necessary to enable the petitioners to protect any pecuniary interest or equity they have.

Judge Thayer delivered the opinion of the court.   The formal entry of the court is as follows:

"The application of Edward S. Harriman, Winslow S. Pierce, and the Oregon Short Line Railroad Company for leave to intervene in this case was heard before this court on April 12 and 13, 1904, and after due consideration it is hereby ordered that the said application be and the same is hereby denied."

After this decision of the circuit court of the United States, the legal contest was shifted from the west to the east; and the history of the Securities case became almost exclusively legal. On petition of Harriman, Pierce, Oregon Short Line Railroad Company, and the Equitable Trust Company of New York,[66] Andrew Kirkpatrick, United States circuit judge, issued an order restraining the Northern Securities Company or any of its officers or agents from disposing of any of its stock until after the hearing and decision upon the motion for a preliminary injunction of Harriman, etc.[67]   The motion and order were made on April 20, 1904, and the hearing set for April 25, 1904, in the city of Trenton, N. J.

The motion for the preliminary injunction is a short document of twenty-five lines, supported by a brief of a little over one hundred pages, supplemented later by a "reply brief" of about the same length.[68]   The brief[69] recites the facts of the organization of the Northern Securities Company, maintains that the court has jurisdiction, repeats that the Securities Company holds the Northern Pacific shares as depository or custodian, denies the alleged equities of the stockholders of the Securities Company, insists upon the illegality of the original transfer of stock to the Securities Company, and presents specific figures expressing the threatened loss to the Harriman interests through the proposed plan of distribution.[70]   The figures show that the annual income which would

---

[66] 36 : 1.
[67] 36 : 4.
[68] 38.
[69] 37.
[70] 37 : 18, 35.

be collected by the Oregon Short Line Company on the proposed distributive shares of the Northern Pacific and Great Northern stock would be $3,969,667, whilst the income which it would collect on the $71,732,062 Northern Pacific stock would be equal to $5,021,244, a difference in annual income of $1,051,577. In general, the brief follows the lines of argument outlined above in connection with the proceedings before the four circuit judges. In fact, from an economic point of view, the case was closed with the supreme court decision of March 14, 1904, although it required another year and a second decision of the supreme court to end the controversy. Familiar facts were rehearsed over and over again, and citations accumulated in geometrical ratio. There may be a great deal in these conflicts between legal giants, representing industrialists of corresponding stature, which possesses value to the student of the principles and technicalities of law; but to a student of economics the interest is not maintained to the end.

On behalf of the Securities Company it was argued [71] that the Northern Pacific stock had been actually sold to and acquired by the Securities Company, that this property (stock) was no longer in existence and could not be restored or returned in kind; that the decree of the trial court does not afford evidence in support of the complainants' bill; that, on the contrary, this decree expressly recognizes the Northern Securities Company as having title to the railway stocks it holds, and the right to distribute them ratably among its stockholders; and that the equities of the stockholders of the Securities Company forbid a restoration of the status quo, even if it were possible to do so, which it is not. The Securities Company also put in evidence depositions of Harriman, Nichols, Hill, and others, chiefly containing facts which have been presented in the earlier chapters of this monograph; as well as the proceedings in court of Chancery of New Jersey, being the case of the Continental Securities Company against the Northern Securities Company.[72] Together, all the briefs of argument and authorities relating to the preliminary injunction amounted to nearly 800 printed pages.

---

[71] **39 and 40.**
[72] **39** : 71-98.

The preliminary injunction asked for was granted, following the hearings of May 20–23, in the circuit court of the United States for the district of New Jersey, by Justice Bradford, July 15, 1904.[73] Justice Bradford stated that the relief prayed for in the petition or bill was in some particulars broader than that granted in the final decree of the trial court, He thought this to be not without significance, "although it is unnecessary now to discuss the point" With respect to some of the alleged facts, important in their bearing upon the equities of the case, the affidavits and exhibits were characterized as conflicting on substantial points, and "the final decision necessarily will involve the consideration of grave, novel and delicate questions of law." The judge did not think the case "ripe for a final decision," the present application being for a preliminary injunction.[74] The granting of a preliminary injunction will not interfere with the operation of the Northern Pacific Railway Company and the Great Northern Railway Company, or either of them, or otherwise prove detrimental to the interests of the public. While it would deprive stockholders for some time from receiving dividends, ample bonds can be provided for their protection.[75] An actual distribution on the pro rata plan, leaving only one per cent of the par value of the outstanding stock of the Northern Securities Company, or $3,954,000, consisting wholly, or practically wholly of property other than stock of both or either of the two railway companies[76] would not only debar the Harriman interests from any relief to which they may be entitled under their present bill, but to a moral certainty entail upon them a burdensome multiplicity of suits attended with great labor and expense.[77] It would also obviously be calculated to hinder, embarrass, and probably or possibly defeat them in their effort to recover large quantities of such stock from persons purchasing the same in good faith and for full consideration, directly or indirectly, from the stockholders of the Northern Securities Company participating in such pro rata distribution, through the creation of new equities on the part of such

[73] 41.
[74] 41 : 20.
[75] 41 : 25.
[76] 41 : 33.
[77] 41 : 26.

purchasers. Whatever action is now taken, it should leave the Harriman interests in a position to enjoy the fruits of their victory in case the final decree should ultimately be determined in their favor. Furthermore, "it is manifestly improper that these matters should be decided on the fragmentary and inconclusive evidence now before the court. * * * This court, as a court of equity, has power so to mold its decrees and to impose such terms as may be necessary to protect the equities of persons who may be affected by its action. * * * Under the circumstances, this court would not be justified in refusing the injunction sought. * * * An interlocutory decree for a preliminary injunction may be prepared and submitted."[78] The order for the injunction was entered August 18, 1904, from which an appeal was taken to the circuit court of appeals for the third circuit.[79] On January 3, 1905, the court of appeals reversed the injunctional order, and thereupon an application was made to the supreme court of the United States for the writ of certiorari, which was granted on January 30, and the matter advanced for hearing, and heard March 1 and 2. The supreme court announced the affirmance of the decree of the circuit court of appeals on March 6, 1905, it being added that an opinion would be filed afterwards.[80]

While the documents in the case before the circuit court of appeals and the United States supreme court were not nearly so voluminous as the records and documents in the earlier cases, they are nevertheless of generous proportions. The second amended bill of complaint covered nearly 450 large printed pages and the briefs in each of the two last cases exceeded 600 pages. In view of the somewhat detailed analysis of the earlier documents which has been presented, these later documents may be passed over with only such notice as may be incidental to the presentation of the main points in the decision of the supreme court which finally terminated this many-sided legal contest. The history of the formation of the Northern Securities Company is recited briefly in several of the later documents, especially in the bill of complaint.[81]

---

[78] 41 : 36-37.
[79] 42 : 10.
[80] 49 : 2, 14.
[81] 35.

CHAPTER IX.

THE FINAL DECISION OF THE SUPREME COURT.

The final decision, as was stated above, was rendered on March 6, 1905. Generally speaking it upheld every important contention of the Northern Securities Company, and the Company has since distributed its stock in accordance with the plan adopted by its stockholders at the meeting of April 21, 1905. Chief Justice Fuller delivered the opinion of the court; and, unlike the decision of March 14, 1904, there were no dissenting opinions.

Taking up the chief contention of the Harriman party, that the Northern Securities Company did not become owner of the Northern Pacific shares, but simply trustee or bailee, and that this claim is justified by the decree of April 9, 1903, the decision of the trial court, Chief Justice Fuller says that the Harriman interests "were not parties of record to that suit, and that they were not parties by representation, if the effect of the transfer as between the parties thereto had been an issue and the vital conflict between complainants and the corporation, now set up, then existed, which would destroy community of interest on which the rule of representation is founded. And, on the other hand, in that suit the Northern Securities Company, at a time when complainant Harriman was a director, answered that: 'Every share of the Great Northern Company and the Northern Pacific Company acquired by this defendant has been, and so long as it remains the property of the defendant will continue to be, held and owned by it in its own right, and not under any agreement, promise, or understanding on its part, or on the part of its stockholders and officers, that the same shall be held, owned or kept by it for any period of time whatever, or under any agreement that in any manner restricts or controls to any extent any use of the same which might lawfully be exercised by any other owner of said stocks.'" The opinion further states that "the circuit court did not determine the quality of the transfer as between the defendants themselves, nor was that the purpose of the government proceedings." After commenting upon certain features of the decree and referring to its terms, he says further: "This did not involve a decision that any original vendor of the railway shares was entitled to a judicial restitution thereof; and such was the view of the circuit court itself." The decree was permissive but not mandatory in its reference to a return of the shares of stock by the Northern Securities Company. The contention of counsel for Harriman that certain expressions in the opinion of Justice Harlan of March 14, 1904, so enlarged the scope of the decree as to give it the effect now attributed to it by the complainants (Harriman, etc.) was characterized as a suggestion "inconsistent with the settled rule that general expressions in an opinion, which are not essential to dispose of a case, are not permitted to control the judgment in subsequent suits." Treating the question as an open one, it seemed to the court "indisputable that, as between these parties, the transaction was one of purchase and sale." In this connection the supreme court confirmed the position of the circuit court of appeals that Harriman himself had distinctly testified that the Northern Pacific stock in question was sold, that he, principally, negotiated the sale; and that there was not attached to the negotiations any condition except as to price. And these statements, said the supreme court, Harriman should not now be permitted to deny as a statement of fact. By the provisions of its charter, the Securities Company had power to buy and sell shares of stock, and, in the discretion of its directors and of the holders of two-thirds of its capital stock, at any time, on notice, to dissolve and to wind up the corporation and distribute its assets. Harriman subjected himself to this power when he accepted the shares of the Northern Securities Company as part payment for his Northern Pacific shares.

"In the present case complainants seek the return of property delivered to the Securities Company pursuant to an executed contract of sale on the ground of the illegality of that contract, but the record discloses no special considerations of equity, justice or public policy, which would justify the courts in relaxing the rigor of the rule which bars a recovery.

"The circuit court decrees put at rest any question that the ratable distribution resolved upon was in violation of public policy.

"And it is clear enough that the delivery to complainants of a majority of the total Northern Pacific stock and a ratable distribution of the remaining assets to the other Securities stockholders would not only be in itself inequitable, but would directly contravene the object of the Sherman law and the purposes of the Government suit.

"The Northern Pacific system, taken in connection with the Burlington system, is competitive with the Union Pacific system, and it seems obvious to us, the entire record considered, that the decree sought by complainants would tend to smother that competition.

"While the superior equities, as against complainants' present claim, of the many holders of Securities shares who purchased in the reliance on the belief that they thereby acquired a ratable interest in all of the assets of the Securities Company, are too plain to be ignored.

"The illegal contract could not be made legal by estoppel, but the ownership of the assets, unaffected by a special interest in complainants, could be placed beyond dispute on their part by their conduct in holding the Securities Company out to the world as unconditional owner.

"And without repeating in detail what has been already set out, it is plain that right of rescission of the executed contract of November 18, 1901, even if rescission could have otherwise been sustained, had been lost by acquiescence and laches at the time this bill was filed.

"Since the transfer of that date Securities stock had passed into the hands of more than 2,500 holders, many of them in Great Britain, France and other parts of Europe; nearly a year after the filing of the government bill 75,000 shares were sold for cash, complainant Harriman concurring; some months after, Harriman and Pierce and the Oregon Short Line Company pledged their 824,000 shares to the Equitable Trust Company; notwithstanding the decree of April 9, 1903, they stood upon their rights as shareholders; and it was not until after March 22, 1904, when defendant's board of directors resolved upon a ratable distribution that complainants undertook to change an election already so pronounced as to be irrevocable in itself in view of the rights of others.

"We regard the contention that complainants are exempt from the doctrine *in pari delicto*, because the parties acted in good faith and without intention to violate the law, as without merit. With knowledge of the facts and of the statute, the parties turned out to be mistaken by supposing that the statute would not be held applicable to the facts. Neither can plead ignorance of the law as against the other, and defendant secured no unfair advantage in retaining the consideration voluntarily delivered for the price agreed.

"Perhaps it should be noticed that the bill sought the return of two parcels of Northern Pacific common stock, the 370,230 shares delivered to the Securities Company, November 18, 1901, and the 347,090 shares received December 27, 1901, from the Northern Pacific Company on the retirement of preferred stock.

"Early in 1901 the Hill-Morgan party held a majority of the common stock, and had asserted the intention to retire the preferred stock, 'without', as Mr. Harriman testified, 'affording the holders of the preferred stock the right to participate in any new securities that might be issued.'

"With full knowledge of that intention the proceedings of the two companies followed in November, 1901, and the absolute and unconditional sale and purchase, as we hold the transaction to have been.

"We find no evidence of any express agreement that complainants should be entitled to the new common stock, and it was certainly not the natural increase of the old stock, but the result of the exercise of the right of subscription. The purchase of the Securities Company was on its own account and not in trust, and cannot be disturbed because of illegal purpose at the clamor of parties *in pari delicto*. And there is here no offer of the restoration of the *status quo,* if that were practicable.

"Doubtless it became the duty of the Securities Company to end a situation that had been adjudged unlawful, and this could be effected by sale and distribution in cash, or by distribution in kind, and the latter method was adopted, and wisely adopted, as we think, for the forced sale of several hundred millions of stock would have manifestly involved disastrous results.

"In fine, the title to those stocks having intentionally been passed, the former owners or part of them cannot reclaim the specific shares and must be content with their ratable proportion of the corporate assets."

CHAPTER X.

CONCLUSIONS.

Whatever conclusions this study may suggest have been indicated in the text, and do not require a re-statement in this brief final chapter. There are a few ideas connected with this study, however, which, as they appear to me to be somewhat fundamental, deserve to be expressed in the closing paragraphs, even at the risk of repetition.

The chief interest of the Northern Securities case lies in the magnitude of the interests involved and in the variety of the economic and legal problems which were incidentally drawn into the controversy. From the point of view of railway organization, the case presents little of consequence, except that railway corporate organization, in the process of metamorphosis or evolution, must avoid the technicality of the particular type of a holding company which the Northern Securities Company represented. From the point of view of railway regulation and the relations between the general public interests and private railway management, the case has no significance whatsoever, in spite of the fact that action against the Securities Company arose out of alleged injurious consequences to the public. It was assumed that competition had been stifled without first asking the question whether competition had actually existed; and whether, if competition could be perpetuated, the public would profit by it. Opposition to the Securities Company rested chiefly upon the same ground that opposition to agreements among railway companies, pools, and all co-operative movements among carriers has generally rested. This undiscriminating opposition to all forms of open concerted action on the part of the railways is in my mind the greatest single blunder in our public policy toward railways. I say "open" concerted action, for every one who knows what is going on is aware of the fact that agreements which rest upon "what each was saying as he looked at his neighbor" have never ceased to exist, and that this form of agreement is the only guarantee against progressive anarchy in railway matters where the law forbids every other form. It is also a fact of common knowledge that such tacit agreements are generally as effective as those which have at times been made known to the public as illegal contracts. I also wish to repeat, what I have expressed heretofore, that I regard the application to railways of the Sherman anti-trust law of 1890 as one of the gravest errors in our legislative history. It is demonstrable that if railway companies had been permitted to co-operate with one another under the supervision of competent public authority, and the Trans-Missouri and Joint Traffic cases had never been decided, the railway situation in the United States would today be appreciably better than it is. However, this is speculation. Nevertheless, even today some legislation which will enable companies to act together under the law, as they now do quietly among themselves outside of the law, is imperative. The American public seems to be unwilling to admit that agreements will and must exist, and that it has a choice between regulated legal agreements and unregulated extra-legal agreements. We should have cast away more than fifty years ago the impossible doctrine of protection of the public by railway competition. We still need a campaign of education on the limitations of competition among public carriers and adequate legislation for the protection of all interests where competition fails.

In expressing these views, I by no means question the motives of the officers of the law who prosecuted the case. Laws should be enforced. The supreme court has said that the Northern Securities Company violated the law, and that should end the matter. But what about the law? Then, too, the prosecution of the Securities case had an undoubted wholesome influence on all great corporations. It was a moral tonic.

From the point of view of railway management, some diversity of opinion existed then and still exists. Able and experienced railway men have expressed the opinion that the Securities Company form of organization is autocratic and narrowing in its effect upon the rank and file; that it restricts the field for honest ambition, and tends to develop excessive dependence upon a very small number of individuals in control. This might not be true in this particular case, they argued, but the system was there which is capable of developing what they objected to. On the other hand, the Securities Company represented greater unity in management and stability in policy. The question arises as to what extent this unity should be developed. The late president of the Southern Pacific believed in one gigantic organization for the whole United States. Few will venture to this length. Two heads working independently of each other are more likely to invent something new or improve the old than one. There can be no question that the preservation of the autonomy of management of a considerable number of companies will ultimately bring about more efficient organization and management on the part of all of them. In this respect, competition can, and should always, endure. However, this is a question for professional railway men rather than for students of the economics of transportation.

A discussion of the results of the case from the purely legal point of view I must leave to the lawyers.

APPENDIX 1.

CERTIFICATE OF INCORPORATION

OF

NORTHERN SECURITIES COMPANY.

We, the undersigned, in order to form a corporation for the purposes hereinafter stated, under and pursuant to the provisions of the Act of the Legislature of the State of New Jersey, "An Act Concerning Corporations (Revision of 1896)," and entitled the Acts amendatory thereof and supplemental thereto, do hereby certify as follows:

FIRST. The name of the corporation is

NORTHERN SECURITIES COMPANY.

SECOND. The location of its principal office in the State of New Jersey is at No. 51, Newark Street, in the City of Hoboken, County of Hudson. The name of the agent therein, and in charge thereof, upon whom process against the corporation may be served, is Hudson Trust Company. Such office is to be the registered office of the corporation.

THIRD. The objects for which the corporation is formed are:

(1) To acquire by purchase, subscription or otherwise, and to hold as investment, any bonds or other securities or evidences of indebtedness, or any shares of capital stock created or issued by any other corporation or corporations, association or associations, of the State of New Jersey or of any other state, territory or country.

(2) To purchase, hold, sell, assign, transfer, mortgage, pledge, or otherwise dispose of, any bonds or other securities or evi-

dences of indebtedness created or issued by any other corporation or corporations, association or associations, of the State of New Jersey, or of any other state, territory or country, and, while owner thereof, to exercise all the rights, powers and privileges of ownership.

(3) To purchase, hold, sell, assign, transfer, mortgage, pledge or otherwise dispose of shares of the capital stock of any other corporation or corporations, association or associations, of the State of New Jersey, or of any other state, territory or country; and, while owner of such stock, to exercise all the rights, powers and privileges of ownership, including the right to vote thereon.

(4) To aid in any manner any corporation or association of which any bonds or other securities or evidences of indebtedness or stock are held by the corporation; and to do any acts or things designed to protect, preserve, improve or enhance the value of any such bonds or other securities or evidences of indebtedness or stock.

(5) To acquire, own and hold such real and personal property as may be necessary or convenient for the transaction of its business.

The business or purpose of the corporation is from time to time to do any one or more of the acts and things herein set forth.

The corporation shall have power to conduct its business in other states and in foreign countries, and to have one or more offices out of this state, and to hold, purchase, mortgage and convey real and personal property out of this state.

FOURTH. The total authorized capital stock of the corporation is Four Hundred Million Dollars ($400,000,000), divided into four million (4,000,000) shares of the par value of one hundred dollars ($100) each. The amount of the capital stock with which the corporation will commence business is thirty thousand dollars.

FIFTH. The names and post office addresses of the incorporators, and the number of shares of stock subscribed for by each (the aggregate of such subscriptions being the amount of capital stock with which this company will commence business) are as follows:

	Number
Name and Post Office Address.	*of shares.*
George F. Baker, Jr., 258 Madison Avenue, New York, New York,...	100
Abram M. Hyatt, 214 Allen Avenue, Allenhurst, New Jersey, ...	100
Richard Trimble, 53 East 25th Street, New York, New York, ...	100

SIXTH. The duration of the corporation shall be perpetual.

SEVENTH. The number of directors of the corporation shall be fixed from time to time by the by-laws; but the number if fixed at more than three, shall be some multiple of three. The directors shall be classified with respect to the time for which they shall severally hold office by dividing them into three classes, each consisting of one-third of the whole number of the board of directors. The directors of the first class shall be elected for a term of one year; the directors of the second class for a term of two years; and the directors of the third class for a term of three years; and at each annual election the successors to the class of directors whose term shall expire in that year shall be elected to hold office for the term of three years, so that the term of office of one class of directors shall expire in each year.

In case of any increase of the number of the directors the additional directors shall be elected as may be provided in the by-laws, by the directors or by the stockholders at an annual or special meeting, and one-third of their number shall be elected for the then unexpired portion of the term of the directors of the first class, one-third of their number for the unexpired portion of the term of the directors of the second class, and one-third of their number for the unexpired portion of the term of the directors of the third class, so that each class of directors shall be increased equally.

In case of any vacancy in any class of directors through death, resignation, disqualification or other cause, the remaining directors, by affirmative vote of a majority of the board of directors, may elect a successor to hold office for the unexpired portion of the term of the director whose place shall be vacant, and until the election of a successor.

The board of directors shall have power to hold their meetings outside the State of New Jersey at such places as from time to time may be designated by the by-laws, or by resolution of the board. The by-laws may prescribe the number of directors necessary to constitute a quorum of the board of directors, which number may be less than a majority of the whole number of the directors.

As authorized by an Act of the Legislature of the State of New Jersey passed March 22, 1901, amending the 17th section of the Act Concerning Corporations (Revision of 1896), any action which theretofore required the consent of the holders of two-thirds of the stock at any meeting after notice to them given, or required their consent in writing to be filed, may be taken upon the consent of, and the consent given and filed by, the holders of two-thirds of the stock of each class represented at such meeting in person or by proxy.

Any officer elected or appointed by the board of directors may be removed at any time by the affirmative vote of a majority of the whole board of directors. Any other officer or employe of the corporation may be removed at any time by vote of the board of directors, or by any committee or superior officer upon whom such power of removal may be conferred by the by-laws, or by vote of the board of directors.

The board of directors, by the affirmative vote of a majority of the whole board, may appoint from the directors an executive committee, of which a majority shall constitute a quorum; and to such extent as shall be provided in the by-laws, such committee shall have and may exercise all or any of the powers of the board of directors, including power to cause the seal of the corporation to be affixed to all papers that may require it.

The board of directors may appoint one or more vice-presidents, one or more assistant treasurers and one or more assistant secretaries; and, to the extent provided in the by-laws, the persons so appointed respectively shall have and may exercise all the powers of the president, of the treasurer, and of the secretary, respectively.

The board of directors shall have power from time to time to fix and to determine and to vary the amount of the working capital of the corporation; to determine whether any, and, if any, what part of any, accumulated profits shall be declared in

7

dividends and paid to the stockholders; to determine the time or times for the declaration and the payment of dividends; and to direct and to determine the use and dispositon of any surplus or net profits over and above the capital stock paid in; and in its discretion the board of directors may use and apply any such surplus or accumulated profits in purchasing or acquiring its bonds or other obligations, or shares of the capital stock of the corporation, to such extent and in such manner and upon such terms as the board of directors shall deem expedient; but shares of such capital stock so purchased or acquired may be resold, unless such shares shall have been retired for the purpose of decreasing the capital stock of the corporation to the extent authorized by law.

The board of directors from time to time shall determine whether and to what extent, and at what time and places, and under what conditions and regulations, the accounts and books of the corporation, or any of them, shall be open to the inspection of the stockholders, and no stockholder shall have any right to inspect any account or book or document of the corporation, except as conferred by statute of the State of New Jersey, or authorized by the board of directors, or by a resolution of the stockholders.

The board of directors may make by-laws, and, from time to time, may alter, amend or repeal any by-laws; but any by-laws made by the board of directors may be altered or repealed by the stockholders at any annual meeting, or at any special meeting, provided notice of such proposed alteration or repeal be included in the notice of the meeting.

IN WITNESS WHEREOF, We have hereunto set our hands and seals, the twelfth day of November, 1901.

GEO. F. BAKER, JR. [L. S.]

ABRAM M. HYATT. [L. S.]

RICHARD TRIMBLE. [L. S.]

Signed, sealed and delivered in the presence of

GEO. HOLMES.

STATE OF NEW YORK,
   County of New York, ⎫
      Manhattan.   ⎬ *ss:*

Be it remembered that on this twelfth day of November, 1901, before the undersigned, personally appeared George F. Baker, Junior, Abram M. Hyatt, Richard Trimble, who, I am satisfied, are the persons named in and who executed the foregoing certificate; and I having first made known to them, and to each of them, the contents thereof, they did each acknowledge that they signed, sealed and delivered the same as their voluntary act and deed.   GEO. HOLMES,

         Master in Chancery of New Jersey.

APPENDIX 2.

STATEMENT OF CARGO FORWARDED ON STEAMSHIP, "MINNESOTA," FROM SEATTLE, JANUARY 23, 1905, IN TONS OF 2,000 LBS.

COMMODITY.	DESTINATION.	TOTAL.
Raw cotton,	Yoho & Kohe,	3735
Wire,	Yoho & Kohe,	107
Leather,	Yoho & Kohe,	139
Machinery,	Yoho & Kohe,	580
Nails,	Yoho & Kohe,	976
P. H. Products,	Yoho & Kohe,	3
Lub oil	Kobo, Japan,	24
Corn,	Yoko, Japan,	33
Barley,	Yoko, Japan,	100
Flat cars,	Yoko, Japan,	704
Lub oil,	Yoko, Japan,	24
Struct. iron,	Yoko, Japan,	12
Rail joints,	Yoko, Japan,	150
Paper,	Yoko, Japan,	20
Leaf tobacco,	Yoko, Japan,	20
Copper,	Yoko, Japan,	336

Total Japan,...6963

C. P. Goods,	Shanghai, China,	1059
Beer,	Shanghai, China,	16
Cigarettes,	Shanghai, China,	227
Leaf tobacco,	Shanghai, China,	40
Nails,	Shanghai, China,	155
Copper,	Shanghai, China,	112
P. H. Products,	Shanghai, China,	227

Total Shanghai,...1836

Wire, ...Hong Kong, China,....... 24

Oats, ... Manila, P. I.,.......... 600
P. H. Products,............. Manila, P. I., ... 5

Total Manila,.................................. 605

Condensed milk,............. various 660
Miscl. Mdse.,................ various 8

Total various,.................................. 668

LOCAL FREIGHT.

Flour, ... 473
Canned salmon,............................... 143
Hay, ... 262
Beer, ... 31
Lumber, ... 79
Miscl. Mdse.,................................ 13

Total local,.................................. 1001

TOTAL CARGO.

Total overland,.............................. 10096
Total local,................................. 1001

.... 11097
Full cargo was 21,000 tons.

APPENDIX 3.

FORM OF CERTIFICATE OF NORTHERN PACIFIC RAILWAY COMPANY PREFERRED STOCK. ....

Shares.　　RAILWAY　　　　　COMPANY.　　Shares.

NORTHERN
PACIFIC

New York　　　　　　　　Certificate.

No.　ooooo　　　　　　　　　　　10 Shares

Preferred Stock.　　　　　Preferred Stock.

This is to certify that ———— is the owner of ten fully paid and nonassessable shares, of the par value of one hundred dollars each in the preferred capital stock of the Northern Pacific Railway Company, transferable only in person, or by attorney, upon the books of the company, at the office of its transfer agents in the city of New York, upon surrender of this certificate. The holders of the preferred stock of the company shall be entitled to noncumulative dividends for each fiscal year, when and as declared by the board of directors of the company, to the extent of four per cent per annum, payable quarterly on the first days of March, June, September, and December, out of any surplus net profits of the company, as determined by said board, before any dividends shall be declared or paid for or in such fiscal year on the common stock, and without deduction for any tax or taxes imposed by the United States or by any state or municipality thereof that the railway company may at any time be required to pay or to retain therefrom. Dividends on the common stock may be declared and paid out of any surplus net profits remaining from any previous fiscal year or years, for which the full dividends at the rate of four per cent per annum shall have been paid on the preferred stock; but after dividends to the extent of four per cent shall have been declared for any one fiscal year on all the stock of the company (common as well as preferred), any further dividends for that fiscal year shall be declared only for the equal ratable benefit of all the stock, whether preferred or common. No dividends shall be paid on the common stock out of surplus net profits of any year for which the full dividends shall not have been paid on the preferred stock. Whenever the full and regular quarterly dividends for two successive quarterly periods after July 1st, 1897, on the preferred stock at the rate of four per cent per annum shall not have been paid in cash, then and in that event at the next annual meeting such number, and only such number, of directors as will constitute a majority of the whole board shall be elected by a separate ballot by the holders of the preferred stock present or represented at such meeting, and the remainder of the board shall be elected by a separate ballot by the holders of the common stock present or represented at such meeting, in every case each share to be entitled to one vote. The company shall not put a mortage upon its property formerly embraced in the system of the Northern Pacific Railroad Company, nor shall the amount of the preferred stock be increased except after obtaining in each instance the consent of the holders of a majority of the whole amount of the preferred stock given at a meeting of the stockholders called for that purpose, and the consent of the holders of a majority of such part of the common stock as shall be represented at such meeting, the holders of each class of stock voting separately. The company shall have the right at its option, and in such manner as it shall determine, to retire the preferred stock in whole or in part, at par, from time to time, upon any first day of January prior to 1917.

All dividends declared on the preferred stock registered in Berlin will be payable there at the rate of 4.20 marks per dollar. This certificate is not valid unless duly registered by the registrar of transfers of the company in the city of New York.

Witness the signatures of the president or one of the vice-presidents of said company, and of J. P. Morgan & Co., its transfer agents in the city of New York.

New York ....

       Transfer agents.

       (Specimen.)

        Vice-president.

STATE OF   WISCONSIN.

Shares $100 each.   Shares $100 each.

Registered:

            CENTRAL TRUST COMPANY OF NEW YORK,

                                            Registrar.

By ——— ———, *Secretary.*

Endorsed:

For value received —— hereby sell, assign, and transfer unto ——— shares of the capital stock represented by the within certificate, and do hereby irrevocably constitute and appoint ——— attorney to transfer the said stock on the books of the within-named company, with full power of substitution in the premises. ——— ———.

Dated, ———, 19—.

APPENDIX 4.

UNDERWRITERS' AGREEMENT.

In presence of ———— ————.

Agreement between Standard Trust Company and certain underwriters, dated November 18, 1901.

Agreement made this 18th day of November, 1901, between the Standard Trust Company of New York (hereinafter called the "Trust Company"), party of the first part, and the other signers of this agreement, or of counterparts thereof (hereinafter called the "Subscribers"), parties of the second part.

The Trust Company, at the request of the subscribers, has made or is about to make an agreement with the Northern Pacific Railway Company of even date herewith (a copy of which is hereto annexed and marked "Exhibit A"), upon the express condition that the subscribers hereto enter into this agreement.

In consideration of the premises, the parties have agreed as follows:

I. The Subscribers hereby severally agree with the Trust Company and with each other to pay to the Trust Company upon its demand, in the proportions set opposite their respective signatures hereto, such sums of money as the Trust Company may from time to time require to meet its obligations under this agreement with the Northern Pacific Railway Company, and the Subscribers further agree in such several proportions to hold the Trust Company harmless from any loss, liability, or expense under or by reason of said agreement with the Northern Pacific Railway Company, or because of any distribution hereunder of the securities to be received by the Trust Company under said agreement.

II. The Subscribers shall severally be entitled to share, in the proportions set opposite their respective signatures hereto, in the benefits of said agreement and in all convertible certificates and common stock of the Northern Pacific Railway

Company which shall remain with the Trust Company after the performance of its obligations under said agreement.

III. The Trust Company shall issue to the Subscribers suitable certificates of participation referring to this agreement, upon which certificates any payments made by the Subscribers shall be endorsed. The Trust Company shall be entitled to reimbursement for its expenses and to reasonable compensation. The written advice of counsel shall be full protection to the Trust Company, as against the Subscribers, for any action it may from time to time take hereunder or in connection with said agreement. This agreement shall bind the executors and administrators of the respective Subscribers.

In witness whereof The Standard Trust Company of New York has caused this instrument to be executed, and its corporate seal to be hereunto affixed by its proper officers, and the parties of the second part have hereunto set their hands the day and year first above written.

THE STANDARD TRUST COMPANY OF NEW YORK,
By Wm. C. Lane, President.

(Corporate Seal.)

Attest: W. C. Cox, Secretary.

Signature of Subscriber.	Proportion of Entire Obligation Taken by Subscriber.
Kuhn, Loeb & Co	One-third (1/3) or twenty-five million dollars ($25,000,000).
J. P. Morgan & Co	One-third (1/3) or twenty-five million dollars ($25,000,000).
Jas. J. Hill	One-ninth 1/9)
Geo. F. Baker	One-ninth 1/9) ⎱ or 1/3.
John S. Kennedy	One-ninth 1/9)

Memorandum of agreement, made this —— day of November, A. D. 1901, by and between Northern Pacific Railway Company, a corporation of the State of Wisconsin, of the first part, and The Standard Trust Company of New York, a corporation of the State of New York (hereinafter termed the "Trust Company"), of the second part.

Witnesseth, that the parties hereto have mutually agreed as follows:

MEYER—HISTORY OF THE NORTHERN SECURITIES CASE.

ARTICLE I.

On January 1, 1902, Northern Pacific Railway Company agrees to sell and to deliver to the Trust Company, and the Trust Company agrees to buy from Northrn Pacific Railway Company, at their face value, all the convertible certificates of indebtedness of the Northern Pacific Railway Company for the aggregate principal sum of seventy-five million dollars ($75,000,000), of the issue authorized by vote of the directors of said company passed November 13, 1901, except such of said certificates as shall be purchased by the holders of the common stock of said corporation, as recited in Article III. of this agreement.

Such convertible certificates are to be dated November 15, 1901, and to be payable on January 1, 1907, in gold coin of the United States of the present standard of weight and fineness, at said company's office in the city of New York, and to bear interest in like gold coin at the rate of four per cent per annum from January 1, 1902, payable semi-annually at said office. Every such certificate shall be convertible into shares of the common stock of the Northern Pacific Railway Company at the rate of one share of one hundred dollars ($100) par value for each one hundred dollars ($100) of the principal of such certificate remaining unpaid at the date of such conversion; and upon surrender to it of any such certificate said Railway Company will issue to the holder of such surrendered certificate shares of its common stock at the rate aforesaid. Such conversion may be made by the Northern Pacific Railway Company, at its option, at any time after November 15, 1901, and shall be made at the demand of any holder of such certificate at any time on or after January 1, 1902. Such certificates shall be in denominations each of one thousand dollars, or some multiple thereof, and shall be substantially of the tenor of the draft thereof, marked "Exhibit A," hereto attached.

Until engraved or lithographed certificates can be prepared, temporary certificates, in form satisfactory to the Trust Company, shall be delivered hereunder, which temporary certificates shall be exchangeable for engraved or lithographed certificates as soon as the same shall be ready for delivery.

ARTICLE II.

Northern Pacific Railway Company covenants and agrees with the Trust Company that all moneys received for such certificates shall be specifically appropriated and used exclusively for the retirement of the preferred stock of the Northern Pacific Railway Company at par, and shall be set apart as a trust fund for such purpose.

ARTICLE III.

It is understood and agreed that suitable opportunity shall be given to every holder of common stock of the Northern Pacific Railway Company registered at the closing of the transfer books on December 10, 1901, to purchase and to pay for, at the price hereinafter stated, an amount of such certificates (subject to a proper adjustment for fractional amounts of certificates) equal to seventy-five eightieths of the par amount of such common stock owned of record by such stockholder.

At any time prior to the sale and delivery of such certificates to the Trust Company, the Northern Pacific Railway Company may sell and deliver, at the price hereinafter stated, to any such holder of common stock, the amount of such certificates which such holder of common stock is to be given such opportunity to purchase; but in case any such sale be made to any stockholder prior to the closing of the transfer books on December 10, 1901, such arrangements shall be made as will prevent any transfer of such stock before the reopening of the transfer books on January 2, 1902, except subject to the condition that the transferees and subesquent holders of such stock prior to such reopening of the transfer books shall release any and all right to purchase any of such certificates from the Northern Pacific Railway Company. As soon as practicable the Northern Pacific Railway Company, by notice, shall extend to each holder of its common stock registered at the closing of the transfer books on Decmeber 10, 1901, suitable opportunity until January 1, 1902, to purchase at the price hereinafter stated an amount of such certificates (subject to adjustment as aforesaid) equal to seventy-five eightieths of the par amount of such common stock owned of record by such stockholder.

After the sale and delivery to the Trust Company of such of said certificates as shall not have been purchased by the stockholders of the Northern Pacific Railway Company, the Trust Company will give to every holder of common stock of said company registered at the closing of the transfer books on December 10, 1901 (other than holders of common stock who previously shall have purchased or shall have had suitable opportunity to purchase a ratable share of such certificates as aforesaid), suitable opportunity, not later than March 1, 1902, to receive on demand, through or from the Trust Company, upon payment to the Trust Company of the price hereinafter stated, an amount of such certificates (subject to adjustment as aforesaid) equal to seventy-five eightieths of the par amount of such common stock owned of record by such stockholder (or a like amount of common stock received upon conversion of such certificates if theretofore converted).

The price payable for all such certificates sold under this article on or before January 1, 1902, shall be a sum equal to the principal thereof. The price payable for all such certificates sold and delivered under this article after January 1, 1902, shall be a sum equal to the principal thereof, and the interest accrued thereon. The price payable for any stock received upon conversion of such certificates shall be the same as the price which would have been payable for a corresponding amount of such certificates.

Under the provisions of this article every such holder of common stock shall only be given the opportunity to purchase, either from the Trust Company or from the Northern Pacific Railway Company, such amount of such certificates (or stock) as in the aggregate shall be equal to seventy-five eightieths of the par amount of the common stock owned of record by such stockholder at the closing of the transfer books on December 10, 1901.

ARTICLE IV.

In case the Northern Pacific Railway Company shall fail to sell and to deliver such certificates to the Trust Company at the times and in the manner herein provided, or shall fail to comply with its agreements herein contained, or in case the Northern Pacific Railway Company shall fail to issue its common stock in exchange for all certificates delivered hereunder to the Trust Company when and as demand therefor shall be made by the Trust Company or other holder, then and in any such case the Trust Company, at its option, by notice delivered at the office of the Northern Pacific Railway Company in the city of New York may forthwith rescind this agreement, and thereupon the Northern Pacific Railway Company, upon surrender to it of any of such certificates, shall be bound to repay to the Trust Company or other holder the price paid for such certificates hereunder, with proper allowance of interest.

This agreement shall be deemed strictly *inter partes,* and shall not give any rights to any person or corporation except the Trust Company and the Northern Pacific Railway Company, except as provided in the certificates themselves.

In witness whereof the parties hereunto have caused these presents to be signed by their officers duly authorized the day and year first above written.

NORTHERN PACIFIC RAILWAY COMPANY,

By ————— —————.

THE STANDARD TRUST COMPANY OF NEW YORK,

By ————— —————.

APPENDIX 5.

NORTHERN PACIFIC RAILWAY COMPANY, DIREC-TORS EIGHTY-THIRD MEETING, NOVEM-BER, 13, 1901.

At a meeting of the board of directors held pursuant to due notice at the office of the company, No. 49, Wall street, New York City, on Wednesday, November 13, 1901, at 2 o'clock p. m., there were present the following newly elected directors (constituting a quorum) viz:

Messrs. Baker, Harriman, Hill, Ives, James, Kennedy, Lamont, Mellen, Rea, Rockefeller, Steele, Stillman, Thomas, Twombly.

On motion Mr. Ives was chosen to act as chairman. He thereupon took the chair and announced the meeting ready for organization.

The secretary then submitted the report of the inspectors of election showing that at the annual meeting of stockholders held on October 1, 1901, the following were elected directors for the ensuing year, to wit:

Robert Bacon, George F. Baker, Edward H. Harriman, James J. Hill, Brayton Ives, D. Willis James, John S. Kennedy, Daniel S. Lamont, Charles S. Mellen, Samuel Rea, William Rockefeller, Charles Steele, James Stillman, Eben B. Thomas, Hamilton McK. Twombly.

The directors then proceeded to the election of officers.

On motion, it was

Resolved, That the secretary be, and hereby he is, directed to cast a ballot in favor of the election of the following-named persons to serve as officers of this company for the ensuing year, towit:

For president, Charles S. Mellen.

For vice-president, Daniel S. Lamont.

For comptroller, Henry A. Gray.

For treasurer, Charles A. Clark.

For secretary and assistant treasurer, George H. Earl.

For assistant secretary, Richard H. Relf.

For general counsel in New York, Francis Lynde Stetson.

For general counsel in Saint Paul, Charles W. Bunn.

The secretary cast the ballot as directed, and the chairman announced that the above-named persons were duly elected to the offices set opposite their names, respectively.

Mr. Ives then resigned the chair in favor of Mr. Mellen.

The resignation of Mr. Robert Bacon as a director of this company was presented, and, on motion, the same was accepted.

Mr. Samuel Spencer was nominated as a director to fill the vacancy caused by the resignation of Mr. Bacon, and on motion, the secretary was directed to cast a ballot in favor of the election of Mr. Spencer. This was done, and the chairman announced that Mr. Samuel Spencer had been duly elected a director of this company to fill the existing vacancy.

On motion of Mr. Steele, it was

Resolved, That the following directors be, and hereby they are, appointed as the executive committee of this company, viz:

Messrs. Baker, Harriman, Hill, Kennedy, Spencer, and the president, or in his absence, the vice-president, exofficio.

The following preamble and resolutions, offered by Mr. Kennedy and seconded by Mr. Baker, were unanimously adopted:

Whereas, under and pursuant to an agreement dated July 13, 1896, the Northern Pacific Railway Company did acquire from Messrs. J. P. Morgan & Co., a copartnership in the city of New York (in said agreement called the Reorganization Managers), certain stocks, bonds, and other property representing the system formerly of the Northern Pacific Railroad Company, and in consideration of such agreement and transfer did issue and deliver to the Reorganization Managers certificates for 750,000 shares of its fully paid and nonassessable preferred stock and 800,000 shares of its fully paid and nonassessable common stock of the character described in a certain plan and agreement for the reorganization of the Northern Pacific Railroad System, dated March 16, 1896; and, furthermore, did agree at all times and in all ways and particulars to cooperate with the Reorganization Managers and assist them in carrying into effect and in accomplishing the purposes of the said plan and agreement of reorganization; and

Whereas in and by the said plan and agreement of reorganization it was expressly provided that the right would be reserved by the new company (being the Northern Pacific Railway Company) to retire this preferred stock in whole or in part at par from time to time upon any first day of January during the twenty years succeeding the date of said reorganization agreement; it being the purpose and the intent of the said agreement that the ultimate control of the new company should be held and be exercised by the holders of the common stock, and that the preferred stock should as soon as practicable be liquidated and be paid off in cash at par; and

Whereas upon the first day of July, 1896, at a meeting of the stockholders of the Northern Pacific Railway Company, each and every stockholder being present and voting in favor thereof, a resolution was duly adopted providing for the issue of $80,000,000 of common stock and of $75,000,000 of preferred stock of the Northern Pacific Railway Company, and expressly prescribing that such preferred stock should be issued upon the condition that at its option the company might retire the same in whole or in part at par, from time to time upon any first day of January prior to 1917; and

Whereas at a meeting of the directors of the Northern Pacific Railway Company, duly held on the 8th day of July, 1896, a form of certificate for the preferred stock of the company, with the conditions and regulations to be incorporated therein or endorsed thereon, was duly adopted by the unanimous vote of the board of directors of the Northern Pacific Railway Company, including the following provision:

"The company shall have the right, at its option, and in such manner as it shall determine, to retire the preferred stock in whole or in part, at par, from time to time on any first day of January prior to 1917;" and

Whereas at a meeting of the stockholders of the Northern Pacific Railway Company, duly held upon July 13, 1896, the said resolution of the board of directors adopting the said form

8

of stock certificate to be issued for the preferred stock was duly ratified and approved by the affirmative vote of every stockholder of the company; and

Whereas each and every certificate for the $75,000,000 of preferred stock of the Northern Pacific Railway Company containing the express provision for the retirement thereof, from time to time thereafter, was issued under and pursuant to the provisions of the said resolution of July 1, 1896, and each and every certificate for stock now outstanding contains such express provision for the retirement thereof; and

Whereas under and pursuant to section 8 of the act, chapter 244 of the private and local laws of Wisconsin, approved April 15, 1895, it was expressly provided that all the affairs of this company should be managed by a board of directors who should be stockholders, and who thereby were invested with all the powers of the corporation save as thereinafter provided; and

Whereas in and by section 11 and section 12 of the said act, chapter 244 of the laws of 1895, it was expressly provided that this company might make its preferred stock convertible into common stock upon such terms and conditions as should be fixed by the board of directors, and that it might in its corporate name execute and deliver its notes, bonds, debentures, or other evidences of indebtedness in such form as from time to time should be prescribed by the board of directors, and in such amount as should be deemed from time to time by said board expedient, and might make the same convertible into its capital stock of any class upon such terms and conditions as to the board of directors might seem advisable; and

Whereas the holders of a majority of the common stock of the Northern Pacific Railway Company have requested the board of directors to take all such action as may be requisite to retire the whole of the preferred stock upon the first day of January, 1902, and have given satisfactory assurances that the necessary moneys for that purpose will be furnished, and that all action requisite for that purpose will be taken by the holders of the common stock, and

Whereas in the judgment of the board of directors of the Northern Pacific Railway Company it is desirable that this com-

pany should now exercise the option to retire the preferred
stock in whole upon the first day of January, 1902:

Now, therefore, it is hereby unanimously

Resolved, (1) That the Northern Pacific Railway Company, in
exercise of its right specifically expressed in each and every
certificate of stock of this company, has determined, and
hereby does determine, to retire the preferred stock of the
Northern Pacific Railway Company, in whole, at par, upon the
first day of January, 1902.

(2)   That notice of the retirement of the preferred stock, substantially in the form of that annexed to the minutes of this
meeting, be published in the manner prescribed by the by-laws
for notice of stockholders' meetings, and that a copy thereof be
mailed to every stockholder of this company.

(3)   That for the purpose of raising the funds necessary to
retire the preferred stock, this company will make and will issue
its negotiable bonds, dated November 15, 1901, for the aggregate principal sum of $75,000,000, payable January 1, 1907, in
gold coin of the United States of the present standard of
weight and fineness, at this company's office in the city of New
York, with interest in like gold coin at the rate of four per
cent per annum from January 1, 1902, payable semi-annually at
said office. Every such bond shall be convertible into shares
of the common stock of this company at the rate of one share of
$100 for each $100 of the principal sum of such bond remaining
unpaid at the date of such conversion; and upon surrender to
it of any such bond this company will issue to the holder of such
surrendered bond shares of this company's common stock at the
rate aforesaid. Such conversion may be made by the company
at its option at any time after November 15, 1901, and shall be
made at the demand of any holder of any such bond at any
time on or after the first day of January, 1902. Such bonds
shall be coupon bonds or registered bonds, in denominations each
of $1,000, or of some multiple thereof, and shall be in such form
as shall be determined by the president or the vice-president of
this company. Every such bond shall be subscribed by the
president or a vice-president and by the secretary or an assistant
secretary and shall be issued under the corporate seal.

(4)   That the president and vice-president of this company,

and each of them, be, and hereby they are, authorized and empowered to contract to sell and to sell all or any of said bonds at a price not less than par and accrued interest; and in such contract to provide for the delivery of all or any part of said bonds upon receiving such payment therefor on or prior to or after December 31, A. D. 1901; and also to covenant and agree that any and all moneys received for said bonds shall be specifically appropriated and used exclusively for the retirement of the preferred stock at par; and accordingly it is hereby expressly declared that all such proceeds shall be set apart and shall be held as a trust fund for such purpose.

Any such contract for delivery of such bonds prior to January 1, 1902, may provide for the payment of the whole or any part of the purchase price of said bonds with allowance of interest, at a rate not exceeding four per cent per annum from the time of the receipt of the price of such bonds until January 1, 1902, the date when such bonds begin to bear interest.

Any and every such contract shall contain a provision giving to the holder of every share of this company's common stock now outstanding suitable opportunity on demand to receive through or from the purchaser of said bonds under said contract, at a price not exceeding par and accrued interest, such bonds (or a like amount of common stock received upon conversion of such bonds, if theretofore converted) to an amount equal to seventy-five eigthtieths of the par amount of said common stock at such time owned by such holder; and for the purpose of providing for subdivision of interests, suitable certificates representing fractional interests in bonds from time to time may be issued, and may be redeemed in such manner as shall be determined by the president or the vice-president.

(5) That the proper officers of this company be, and hereby they are, directed, out of the proceeds of said bonds, and out of any other moneys in the company's treasury available for that purpose, pay at the company's New York office, to each holder of record of the preferred stock of this company, on and after January 1, 1902, upon surrender of the certificates for such stock, $100 for each and every of the shares of preferred stock for which the certificates shall be so surrendered.

(6) That all of the preferred stock of this company be, and

hereby it is, declared to be retired from and after December 31, A. D. 1901, and that from and after that date all of the authorized capital stock of this company, fixed at $155,000,000, by resolution of this company's stockholders at the meeting thereof held on the first day of July, 1896, be of one kind and be without preference in favor of any part thereof, and the total authorized capitalized stock of this company continue to be $155,000,000, as so fixed at said meeting.

(7)   That the president, the vice-president, the treasurer, and the secretary of the Northern Pacific Railway Company be, and hereby they are, authorized from time to time to take all proceedings and to do all acts necessary or suitable to carry these resolutions fully into effect.

(8)   That for the purpose of the retirement of the preferred stock, the transfer books of the stock of this company be closed at three o'clock p. m. on Tuesday, December 10, 1901, and that the transfer books of the common stock be reopened upon Thursday, January 2, 1902, at ten o'clock a. m.

On motion, the following resolutions were adopted:

Resolved, That the action of the executive committee in declaring from the net earnings of this company a dividend of one per cent on the preferred stock of this company, to be paid December 5, 1901, to the holders of record of preferred stock at the closing of the transfer books on November 8, 1901, be, and hereby the same is, ratified and confirmed.

Resolved, That there be, and hereby there is, declared from the net earnings of this company a final dividend of one per cent on the preferred stock of this company, the same to be paid on or after January 1, 1902, to the holders of record at three o'clock p. m. on Tuesday, December 10, 1901, at which time the transfer books are to be closed for the retirement of the preferred stock under the resolutions of this company.

The executive committee reported by the reading of the minutes of its meetings held October 7th and 21st and November 4th, 1901, and on motion the committee's action as reported was approved, ratified and confirmed.

On motion, it was

Resolved, That the following treasury securities be sold to the

Northwestern Improvement Company as of October 31, 1901, at and for the prices named, to wit:

$330,000.00	prior lien bonds at 105	$346,500.00
1,800,000.00	general lien bonds at 70	1,260,000.00
260,000.00	St. Paul-Duluth Div. bonds at 100..	260,000.00
9,000.00	Minnesota transfer bonds at 100...	9,000.00
2,000,000.00	N. W. Improvebent Co. stock at 75.	1,500,000.00
2,245,000.00	Wash. and Col. River Ry. inc. bonds at 40	898,000.00
280,000.00	Washington Central bonds at 90...	252,000.00
323,183.64	Montana R. R. notes.............	323,183.64
381,992.24	Minn. and International notes.....	381,992.24
762,393.01	Brainerd and No. Minn. notes.....	762,393.01

8,391,568.89   5,993,068.89

On motion, it was

Resolved, That the action of the president of this company in executing, and the action of the assistant secretary, R. H. Relf, in executing, attesting, and affixing the corporate seal to a certain bond on behalf of this company as principal, and Charles S. Mellen and Daniel S. Lamont, as sureties unto the United States of America for twenty-five thousand dollars, covering northerly 350 feet of Ocean Warehouse No. 1, situate on the water front at Tacoma, Washington, which bond bears date November 4, 1901, are hereby fully ratified and confirmed, and said bond is made hereby the valid obligation of this company.

The president submitted a map, in duplicate, of the definite location of an extension of this company's Gaylord and Ruby Valley Branch, from a point in the north line of section 34, township 3 south, range 6 west, of Montana principal meridian, thence in a generally southeasterly direction to and up the valley of the Ruby River, and to a point in the south line of section 9, township 6 south, range 4 west, of the same meridian, a distance of 19.17 miles, all in Madison County, Montana.

On motion, it was

Resolved, That the map this day submitted showing the line of route of the extension of this company's Gaylord and Ruby

Valley branch be, and the same is hereby, adopted as the route of definite location of the extension of said branch.

On motion, it was

Resolved, That the Standard Trust Company of New York, as trustee under the trust indenture securing Northern Pacific-Great Northern, C., B. and Q. collateral 4 per cent joint bonds, dated July 1, 1901, be, and hereby is, authorized to cremate from time to time, in the presence of this company's representative, coupon bonds issued under said trust indenture received and cancelled by said trustee in exchange for registered bond certificates issued under said trust indenture, provided that the said trustee shall thereupon deliver to this company a certificate of such cremation in satisfactory form, which certificate shall be accepted by this company as the delivery of the cancelled coupon bonds prescribed by section 4 of article one of said trust indenture.

On motion, it was

Resolved, That the Farmers' Loan and Trust Company, as trustee under the general second, general third, and consolidated mortgages of the Northern Pacific Railroad Company, be, and hereby is, authorized to cremate, in the presence of this company's representative, coupon bonds issued under any of said mortgages received and cancelled by said trustee in exchange for registered bond certificates issued under said mortgages, and to cremate in like manner all coupon bonds now in its possession engraved for issuance but never issued.

On motion, it was

Resolved, That the action of the president in selling to the insurance fund the securities below mentioned be, and the same is hereby, approved, to wit:

$39.000 Northern Pacific Railway Co. general lien 3 per cent.
  bonds, at 70... $27,300
$7,000 Northern Pacific Railway Co. prior lien 4 per cent
  bonds, at 105.. 7,350
$9,000 Northern Pacific Railway Co. St. Paul-Duluth Division
  4 per cent bonds, at 100.................................. 9,000
$6,000 Washington Central Railway Co. 4 per cent. bonds, at 90   5,400

$49,050

BULLETIN OF THE UNIVERSITY OF WISCONSIN.

The treasurer's statement showing average bank balances for the quarter ending September 30, 1901, was submitted and ordered filed.

The following schedules showing the execution of deeds, leases, and miscellaneous documents during September, 1901, were submitted:

Schedule of land department deeds executed by the Northern Pacific Railway Company, aggregating 60,446.62 acres, for $117,926.14.

Schedule of land department deeds executed by the Northwestern Improvement Company, aggregating 15,802.04 acres, for $43,806.71.

Schedule of leases of right of way and other operating department property.

Statement of miscellaneous deeds, contracts, and relinquishments.

Schedule of land department leases executed by the Northern Pacific Railway Company, western division.

On motion, the execution of deeds, leases, etc., this day reported was approved, ratified, and confirmed.

The following schedules showing the execution of deeds, leases, and miscellaneous documents during October, 1901, were submitted:

Schedule of land department deeds executed by the Northern Pacific Railway Company, aggregating 80,648.94 acres, for $168,323.34.

Schedule of land department deeds executed by the Northwestern Improvement Company, aggregating 24,017.66 acres, for $50,007.35.

Schedule of leases of right of way and other operating department property.

Statement of miscellaneous deeds, contracts, and relinquishments.

Schedule of land department leases executed by the Northern Pacific Railway Company and the Northwestern Improvement Company.

On motion, the execution of deeds, leases, etc., this day reported was approved, ratified, and confirmed.

On motion, the meeting then adjourned.

GEO. H. EARL, *Secretary.*

APPENDIX 6.

CIRCULAR LETTER TO GREAT NORTHERN STOCKHOLDERS.

The following is a copy of a circular issued by the Northern Securities Company, November 22, 1901, to holders of stock of the Great Northern Railway Company.

[Northern Securities Company. James J. Hill, president; John S. Kennedy, first vice-president; George F. Baker, second vice-president; D. Willis James, third vice-president; W. P. Clough, fourth vice- president; E. T. Nichols, secretary and treasurer.]

27–29 PINE STREET,
New York City, November 22nd, 1901.
To holders of stock of the Great Northern Railway Company:

The Northern Securities Company, incorporated under the laws of the State of New Jersey, with an authorized capital stock of $400,000,000, and with power to invest in and hold the securities of other companies, has commenced business, and has acquired from several large holders of stock of the Great Northern Railway Company a considerable amount of that stock.

A unifrom price has been paid of $180 per share, in the fully paid stock of this company, at par. This company is ready to purchase additional shares of the same stock at the same price, payable in the same manner, and will accept offers made on that basis if made within the next sixty days.

Offers for sale of stock of the Great Northern Railway Company should be made upon the enclosed form, and should be accompanied by the certificates of the stock offered with transfers duly executed, having United States stamps for transfer tax of two cents per share affixed.

Upon receipt of any such offer, so accompanied, the Northern Securities Company will deliver to the seller of the stock of the Great Northern Railway Company certificates of its own stock to the amount of the purchase price above named, or, if such certificates are not then ready for delivery, its negotiable receipt obliging it to issue and deliver such certificates as soon as ready. For fractional parts of shares scrip certificates convertible into stock in multiples of $100 will be given.

NORTHERN SECURITIES COMPANY,
By JAMES J. HILL, President.

To the NORTHERN SECURITIES COMPANY,

New York:

The subscribers hereby offer to sell and deliver to the Northern Securities Company ———— shares in the capital stock of the Great Northern Railway Company, represented by the certificates hereto attached, for the price of one hundred and eighty dollars ($180) per share, payable in the fully paid stock of the Northern Securities Company, at par, in accordance with the terms of the circular of the latter-named company, dated November 22nd, 1901.

The stock of the Northern Securities Company to be paid in accordance with the foregoing tender should be issued as follows:

Shares.	Name.	Full address.
....	....	....
....	....	....
....	....	....

Dated ————————, 190——.

APPENDIX 7.

CIRCULAR ON DISTRIBUTION OF STOCK.

NORTHERN SECURITIES COMPANY.

Directors.

Daniel S. Lamont,	Robert Bacon,
John S. Kennedy,	George F. Baker,
Edward T. Nichols,	George C. Clark,
George W. Perkins,	William P. Clough,
Jacob H. Schiff,	Edward H. Harriman,
James Stillman,	James J. Hill,
Nicholas Terhune,	D. Willis James,

Samuel Thorne.

26 Liberty Street,
New York, March 22, 1904.

To the Stockholders of the Northern Securities Company:

Since the formation of your company with a view of promoting, developing and enlarging the commerce and traffic of the country served by the Great Northern and Northern Pacific Railway Companies, and by the Chicago, Burlington and Quincy Railroad Company, the traffic and earnings of the three railways have largely increased. Rates paid by the public have been materially reduced. The respective railways have been extended and their condition and facilities improved and increased.

The stock of the Northern Securities Company was issued solely for the shares of the Northern Pacific and Great Northern Railway Companies, and other properties purchased by it.

In forming the company and disposing of its shares, no commissions were paid nor has the company incurred any expenses save those necessary for obtaining its charter, and for the economical conduct of its affairs.

The company's acquisition of Northern Pacific and Great Northern shares was made in the full belief that such purchases were in no wise obnoxious to any law of the United States—an opinion which has received the approval of four justices of the supreme court of the United States, namely, Mr. Chief Justice Fuller, and Associate Justices Edward D. White, Rufus W. Peckham and Iliver Wendell Holmes, in the suit brought by the United States against the right of the company to hold and vote the shares. However, the majority of the court, disregarding as irrelevant any beneficial increase of commerce, was of the opinion, that as a matter of law your company's holding of the stocks of the two railway companies in itself constituted a restraint of interstate commerce prohibited by the so-called Sherman Act of 1890. Accordingly the railway companies have been forbidden to permit your company to vote or to collect dividends on the shares held by it.

Therefore, your directors, at a meeting held this day, have, under advice of counsel, decided that in order to fully and promptly comply with the decree in this suit, it is necessary to reduce the capital stock of the company, and to distribute to its shareholders the shares of stock of said railway companies now held by it.

To this end they have adopted resolutions recommending to the stockholders

First. That the capital stock of this company be reduced from 3,954,000 shares, now outstanding, to 39,540 shares, being a reduction of 99 per centum.

Second. That said 99 per cent. of the present outstanding shares be called in for surrender and cancellation.

Third. That against each share of the stock of this company so to be surrendered, there will be delivered

$39.27 stock of the Northern Pacific Railway Company,

$30.17 stock of the Great Northern Railway Company,

and proportionate amounts thereof for each fraction of a share of stock of this company so to be surrendered.

As required by the laws of the State of New Jersey, under which the company was created, a special meeting of the shareholders of this company has been called by the board of directors, for Thursday, April 21, 1904, at eleven o'clock in the forenoon, at the office of the company, 51 Newark Street, Hoboken, N. J., to vote upon said resolutions and upon such other business as may be brought before said meeting.

For the purpose of this meeting, the stock transfer books will be closed April 18, 1904, at three o'clock P. M.

Holders of this company's stock to a large extent have already expressed their approval of the recommendations of the board, but the laws of New Jersey require a two-thirds vote of the shareholders to permit the company to reduce its capital stock. Such vote is the first step necessary for the proposed distribution of the railway companies' shares. The collection of the May and subsequent dividends on such shares being forbidden by the decree until such distribution has been made, the importance of promptly executing and forwarding proxies is obvious.

The assets of the company remaining in its treasury after the foregoing distribution is made, will consist of stocks and other property in no way involved in the suit, producing income, and conservatively valued at an amount in excess of the $3,954,000, to which it is proposed to reduce the stock of your company.

Notice of the due approval by the special meeting of the recommendations of the board of directors will be immediately published, whereupon, stockholders should deliver their *entire* holdings of stock at this office promptly on and after April 23, 1904. Against such delivery, certificates for the one per centum thereof to be retained by stockholders, will be returned to them, together with the amount of stock of each of said railway companies, to which they may become entitled as above, on account of the ninety-nine per centum of their holdings of Northern Securities stock surrendered for cancellation. Fractional parts of shares will be adjusted by the delivery of scrip certificates.

All stock surrendered must be fully executed for transfer, either upon the certificates or upon an attached power of transfer.

By order of the board of directors,

JAMES J. HILL,
President.
EDWARD T. NICHOLS,
Secretary.

APPENDIX 8.

LETTER TO STOCKHOLDERS.

NORTHERN SECURITIES COMPANY,
26 Liberty Street,

New York, June 11, 1904.

To the Stockholders:

A circular recommending reduction of the capital stock of this company and a ratable distribution of its railway shares as surplus assets was issued March 22, 1904.

Shortly thereafter Messrs. Harriman and Pierce and the Oregon Short Line Railroad Company petitioned the circuit court for the District of Minnesota for leave to intervene in the suit of the United States against this company, asking that this company should deliver to them $78,108,000 stock of the Northern Pacific Railway Company (part of the common assets of this company), instead of their ratable proportion of such assets as proposed by your directors in that circular. The court denied the petition.

About the same time, another suit on similar grounds was brought against this company in the Court of Chancery of the State of New Jersey by the Continental Securities Company, Clarence H. Venner, president. In this suit an injunction was asked forbidding the holding of your special meeting called for April 21, 1904.

The court refused to grant the injunction, holding that this company had title to the stocks of the Northern Pacific and Great Northern Railway Companies, that their proposed distribution was in conformity with the laws of New Jersey (the State in which this company is incorporated), and in no way violative of the decrees of the United States court.

On the 20th of April, 1904, Messrs, Harriman and Pierce and the Oregon Short Line Railroad Company began another suit against this company in the circuit court of the United States for the District of New Jersey, on grounds, and making claims, similar to those in their application in the State of Minnesota. In this case there has been a hearing on plaintiff's motion for a preliminary injunction to restrain this company from parting with the particular stock claimed by them. An early decision on this motion is expected.

The special meeting of stockholders was held April 21, 1904. Those present, representing nearly 75 per cent of the capital stock of the company, unanimously adopted resolutions reducing its stock to $3,954,000, and providing for the ratable distribution of its railway shares as surplus assets recommended by your directors in the circular of March 22, 1904.

The Northern Pacific and Great Northern Railway Companies declared, at the usual dates, quarterly dividends of 1¾ per cent on their respective shares, payable May 2, 1904, to those persons in whom the title to such shares shall be found to vest.

Cash to pay these dividends has been set apart and deposited in bank for that purpose by both railway companies and payment thereof will immediately follow the distribution and formal transfer of the railway shares.

Your company is advised that the earnings and income of the railway companies in which it is interested as a stockholder continue satisfactory.

Respectfully,
JAMES J. HILL,
President.

APPENDIX 9.

BALANCE SHEET.

NORTHERN SECURITIES COMPANY,

26 Liberty Street, New York.

To the Stockholders of the Northern Securities Company:

The reduction of the company's capital stock from $395,400,000 to $3,954,000, made by the amendment to its Certificate of Incorporation adopted by the stockholders at their special meeting held on April 21, 1904, having in all respects been sustained by the unanimous decision of the supreme court of the United States, became finally effective from and after April 18, 1905, by the filing, on that date, in the proper office of the State of New Jersey, of the Certificate of Amendment.

The *pro rata* distribution of the company's holdings of Northern Pacific and Great Northern shares, in process of carrying out the reduction of its own capital stock, has substantially been completed. Considerably less than one-hundredth part of one per cent of the company's original stock, held in small, scattered lots, remains to be surrendered.

From the company's remaining assets, represented by its reduced capital stock, it has received, during the current business year, ending December 31, 1905, income sufficient to permit payment to holders of that stock of a dividend of five per centum upon the amount thereof.

Your board of directors has accordingly declared a dividend at that rate, payable on January 10, 1906, to holders of record on that date of shares of the reduced capital stock.

For your information herewith are transmitted a revenue account, a general statement of transactions and a balance sheet, prepared by the company's secretary and treasurer, affording, in concise form, a complete view of the company's business operations from the commencement to the present date.

By order of the Board of Directors,

JAMES J. HILL,

December 31, 1905.   *President.*

NORTHERN SECURITIES COMPANY.

Revenue account from November 13, 1901 (date of organization), to December 31, 1905.

To taxes paid—State of New Jersey...... $85,179 09		
State of New York 449 93		
United States—On origin-al issue of stock....... 174,285 51		
	$259,914 53	
To interest and exchange..........	186,685 69	
To expense of administration.	264,039 76	
To legal expenses	595,420 71	
To dividends paid on stock of Northern Securities Co.	36,299,620 63	
To balance, surplus revenue carried to profit and loss account....... g	2,281,007 20	
	$39,886,688 52	
By dividends collected on stocks belonging to the company..........................		$39,886,688 52
		$39,886,688 52

Balance sheet, December 31, 1905.

To organization expense (including $80,000 incorporation fee paid to the state of New Jersey) ....p	$85,048 35	
To investments: Stocks now owned other than Northern Pacific and Great Northern......... o	6,047,606 73	
To cash.... r	420,768 20	
	$6,553,423 28	
By capital stock..... f		$3,954,000 00
By profit and loss:		
Surplus revenue.........g $2,281,007 20		
Premium on 75,220 shares stock of Northern Securities Co. sold in market....h 838,902 50		
Northern Securities stock bought and cancelled.... b $2,643 75		
Less cash cost of same....bi 2,379 02		
264 73		
Profit on Nor. Pac. and Gt. Northern stock sold..... m & n 70,996 95		
$3,191,171 38		
Deduct value of Nor. Pac. and Gt.N. stocks distributed to Nor. Sec. stockholders under resolution of April 21, 1904.......j & k. $392,037,748 10		
Less Nor. Sec. stock retired against that distribution .....l 391,446,000 00	$591,748 10	
		$2,599,423 28
		$6,553,423 28

f Capital stock represents 1 per cent of the old capital stock of $395,400,000 of which 99 per cent ($391,446,000) was retired when the stockholder's resolution of April 21, 1904, went into effect. Certificates for $27,100 of the old stock remain outstanding. One per cent. of this amount ($271) is included in the $3,954,000 of present capital stock. The remaining 99 per cent thereof ($26,829) was retired by the resolutions of April 21, 1904, and now represents a claim upon the Northern Securities Company for $10,535.83 Northern Pacific stock and $8,094.41 Great Northern stock, which stocks the Northern Securities Company holds for delivery upon surrender to it of the old Northern Securities certificates.

9

Statement showing issuance of capital stock and its subsequent reduction; application of capital stock and of its cash proceeds; funds derived from other sources; purchase of securities, their cost and how provided for; other disbursements; final disposition of Northern Pacific and Great Northern stocks under stockholder's resolutions of April 21, 1904, and otherwise.

	Cost	How Paid For	
		Stock of N. S. Co.	Cash
Investments:			
c410,850 shares N. P. pfd. (H. & P. purchase)	$41,085,000 00	$32,169,371 00	$8,915,629 00
370,230 shares N. P. Com. (H. & P. Purchase) ... x	50,322,500 00	50,322,500 00	
Total price paid to H. & P.	$91,407,500 00	$82,491,871 00	$8,915,629 00
820,273.625 shares N. P. stock @ 115 per cent. ... x	94,331,467 75	94,331,122 75	345 00
347,090,625 shares N. P. stock obtained from N. P. Ry. Co. in exchange for $34,709,062.50 N. P. convertible bonds bought at par for cash.... x	34,709,062 50		34,709,062 50
Total, 1,537,594 25 shares costing ... x $179,363,030 25			
Less, 1,537,594.25 shares disposed of for ... d 179,403,551 44			
Excess proceeds to P. & L. account ... m $40,521 19			
1,172,542.50 shares G. N. Pfd. @ 180 per cent. ...	$212,764,850 00	211,057,650 00	1,707,200 00
8,700.00 shares G. N. Pfd. bought for cash ...			
Total, 1,181,242.50 shares costing ... e $212,764,850 00			
Less, 1,181,242.50 shares disposed of for ... e 212,795,325 76			
Excess proceeds to P. & L. account ... n $30,475 76			
Other stocks purchased ... 0	6,047,606 73		6,047,606 73
Gross cost of investments ...	$439,260,486 98	$387,880,643 75	$51,379,843 23
Deduct proceeds investments contra ... c, d, & e $433,283,877 20	$433,212,880 25	a	
Less profit on N. P. and Gt. N. stocks ... 70,996 95			
Net cost of "other stocks" ...	$6,047,606 73		
Organization expense ...			p 85,048 35
Cost of $2,643.75 N. S. stock bought and cancelled (see contra) to reduce stock to even amount ...			bi 2,379 02
			r 420,768 20
Cash in treasury—see balance sheet ...			$51,888,038

		Cash.
Capital stock:		
Issued to incorporators at par for cash	$30,000 00	$30,000 00
Issued and sold in market to pay for 8,700 shares Gt. N. stock	1,557,400 00	1,721,894 25
Issued and sold in market for general purposes	5,934,600 00	6,609,008 25
Total capital stock sold for cash	$7,522,000 00	$8,360,902 50
Issued for property per statement contra .... *a*	387,880,643 75 *h*	
Total capital stock issued	$395,402,643 75	
Less: Purchased in market (see contra) and cancelled to reduce stock to even amount.*b* $2,643 75		
Retired by stockholders' resolutions of April 21, 1901 ....*l* 391,446,000 00	391,448,643 75	
Reduced capital stock now outstanding ....*f*	$3,954,000 00	
Securities disposed of:		
Nor. Pac. Pfd. stock—410,850 shares redeemed by N. P. Ry. Co. at par for cash		41,085,000 00 *c*
Nor. Pac. stock 385,8838 shares sold for cash	$85,582 28	85,582 28 *j*
1,537,208.3662 shares distributed at cost	179,317,969 16	
Total........... 1,537,594.25 shares disposed of for	$179,403,551 44	*d*
Gt. Nor. Pfd. stock 249,9982 shares sold for cash	$75,546 82	75,546 82 *k*
1,180,992.5018 shares distributed at cost	212,719,778 94	
Total........... 1,181,242.50 shares disposed of for	$212,795,325 76	*e*
Surplus revenue		2,281,007 20 *g*
		$51,888,038 80

Having made an audit of the accounts from the organization of the company to December 31, 1905, and verified cash on hand, securities owned and capital stock outstanding, we certify that in our opinion the foregoing revenue account, balance sheet and related general statement are correct.

THE AUDIT COMPANY OF NEW YORK,
By E. T. PERINE, *General Manager.*

EDWARD T. NICHOLS, *Secretary and Treasurer.*

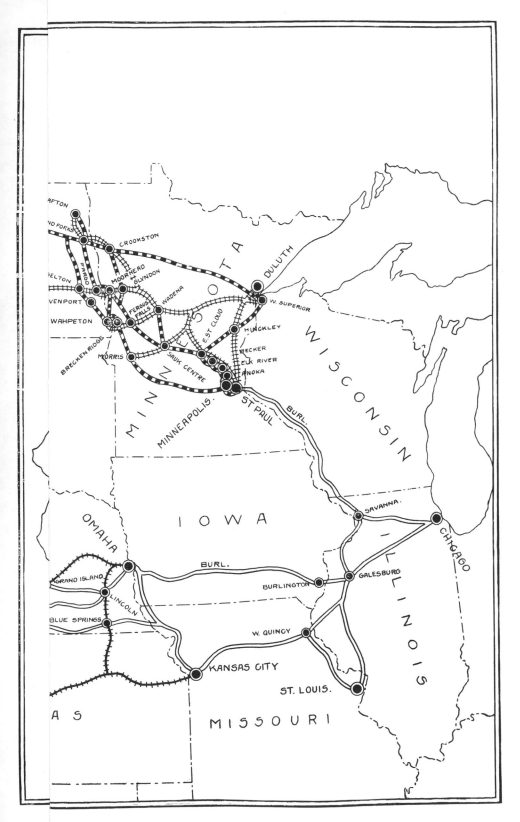

INDEX.

INDEX.

INDEX.